PENGUIN BUSINESS

THE HABIT OF WINNING

Prakash Iyer is a former CEO-turned-best-selling author and motivational speaker. He is also a certified leadership coach—and an uncertified cricket junkie.

In his last role, he was the managing director of Kimberly-Clark Lever. Earlier roles include CEO of Infomedia India Limited and executive director at PepsiCo. An alumnus of IIM Ahmedabad, he started his career with Hindustan Unilever Limited.

Passionate about cricket—and people—Prakash speaks and writes extensively on motivation, leadership, teamwork and winning. his second book, *The Secret of Leadership*, was also published by Penguin random house and is a national bestseller.

You can reach him at pi@prakashiyer.com.

PRAKASH IYER

Foreword by R. Gopalakrishnan

THE HABIT OF WINNING

Stories to INSPIRE, MOTIVATE *and Unleash the* WINNER WITHIN

BUSINESS
An imprint of Penguin Random House

PENGUIN BUSINESS

USA | Canada | UK | Ireland | Australia
New Zealand | India | South Africa | China

Penguin Business is part of the Penguin Random House group of companies whose addresses can be found at global.penguinrandomhouse.com

Published by Penguin Random House India Pvt. Ltd
4th Floor, Capital Tower 1, MG Road,
Gurugram 122 002, Haryana, India

Penguin
Random House
India

First published by Penguin Books India 2011
Published in Portfolio 2013
Published in Penguin Business 2023

First published by Penguin Books India 2011
Published in Portfolio 2013

53 52 51 50 49

The views and opinions expressed in this book are the author's own and the facts are as reported by him which have been verified to the extent possible, and the publishers are not in any way liable for the same.

ISBN 9780143420866

Typeset in Dante MT by SÜRYA, New Delhi
Printed at Replika Press Pvt. Ltd, India

www.penguin.co.in

MIX
Paper from
responsible sources
FSC
www.fsc.org
FSC® C016779

To Mom and Dad

'Winning is a habit.
Unfortunately, so is losing.'

—Vince Lombardi

Contents

III: PERSEVERANCE

IV: WINNER'S MINDSETS

V: GIVING

VI: HARD WORK

VII: THE WINNER'S WAY

VIII: WINNING WITH TEAMS

IX: OTHER PEOPLE

X: FINDING BALANCE

XI: TAKE ACTION

Foreword

I have known Prakash as a young lad in Unilever where we worked together for several years. It has been a privilege seeing him evolve from a successful manager to an inspiring leader. It would have been disappointing had he not decided to further disseminate the insights he has gained through years of leading teams across different companies and challenging circumstances. I am glad that he has chosen to do so through this delightful book full of stories and anecdotes. In a very charming and non-prescriptive manner, the book stimulates the reader to reflect on what it takes to be a successful manager and leader. These nuggets of management draw significant lessons from nature, sports and episodes from daily lives and thus are easy to relate to.

There are two schools of thought on leadership, one strong view being that leadership is innate and cannot be taught, while the other school strongly believes that leadership can be learnt. Prakash obviously belongs to the latter group and so do I. Even the clan which believes leadership can be learnt is split into two sub-clans. While one strongly relies on techniques and processes to influence its students, the other believes in shifting the onus on to the students to do the learning themselves. The prerequisite for the latter, however, involves creation of an environment that brings in engagement, immersion, reflection and contemplation. I am a strong proponent of the latter and surely Prakash subscribes to the same view. It is evident that storytelling creates a connect with the audience and is a perfect mechanism to foster reflection. The strong connection between learning and stories exist because in anecdotes, an idea is united with an emotion. Prakash has weaved a string of stories which put together practically covers all that budding managers need to imbibe to transform themselves into future leaders and winners.

In the 1940s, the great Indian statesman and politician C. Rajgopalachari wrote a series of weekly chapters on the great Indian epics, the Ramayana and the Mahabharata. These were finally put together as an enduring book. To this day, the book sells very well. Its longevity demonstrates the value and durability of stories and emotions. Think of the best lessons you have learnt in professional or personal lives. Almost always, the lesson is mostly associated with an anecdote from your experience or an interaction with somebody you respect or a story told by somebody. There are traditions of storytelling in India that have evolved over the centuries; for example, the jatra in rural Bengal, the Upanyasam in Tamil Nadu, and the harikatha in the north are regional expressions of education and entertainment rolled into one. This is so in other countries too.

The drama of human emotion is a great preservative for ideas, because both the idea and the drama get indelibly etched in your mind. Storytelling is not normally a welcome skill in management; in fact it is pejorative. But thanks to efforts by authors like Prakash, narrative and anecdotal style is gaining prominence to simplify and demystify the esoteric world of management. This is done in a manner that profound lessons are imparted with such poise and elegance that they stay with the reader. The book is fast, pacy and one-flight long but leaves enough for the reader to reflect long after completing the book.

Normally, books in this genre tell us what to do and how to do it. Refreshingly enough, this book also tells us when to stand still. I am referring to my favourite story from the book, which like other stories, leaves us with a lot to think about. In the story, the author talks about a piece of research by a team of scholars in Israel who wanted to study a soccer goalkeeper's mindset in a penalty shoot. After analysing a number of penalty kicks from major league games, the conclusion they reached was that a goalkeeper's best chance of blocking a penalty kick is to stay put at the centre. Despite this, in 92 per cent of the cases, the goalkeeper committed himself to a dive on either side! The answer lies in the bias for action that high achievers have, whether in a game of soccer or life in general. When standing still can perhaps fetch the desired result, the 'dive' on either side demonstrates the desire to be seen as somebody who at least tried. Standing still is scorned at when that could have been the most effective route. The author then gives practical instances of how deeply this bias runs when we look around: some of the most memorable advertising campaigns being stopped by a new brand manager so that he is seen doing something of his own, CEOs busy acquiring businesses, divesting, downsizing, etc. when doing nothing could have been the best course of action!

On similar lines, the author narrates a fantastic story of a football coach who on the first day of practice came without a football. The students were uneasy but the coach had an indisputable logic. At any point in time, only one man has the ball in a football game. It is important to learn what the remaining twenty-one should do and for that one doesn't need a football! The urge to control the ball by every player can lead to disaster and thus team work needs to be practised from day one!

In all forms of organizations, managers face leadership issues for which they seek solutions. In the earlier part of one's professional career, one is dealing with known issues and known solutions. The intensity of ambiguity increases with higher leadership roles and the most complex issues that we eventually start facing are unknown issues having unknown solutions. Thus, the prime challenge of future leadership is to understand the root causes of ambiguity. In a climate of uncertainty, leaders look for maps on how to get from one place to a target destination. Psychologist Karl Weick has pointed out that maps can help in known worlds which have been charted before. Where the world has not been charted, the compass is required, he argues, because amidst uncertainty, it gives you a general sense of direction. Therefore, navigating the leadership ocean requires both the compass and the map. Thus, while maps which are equivalent to the factual, functional and analytical knowledge can help us deal with relatively known problems, what differentiates leaders from others is the ability to deal with complex issues where maps will not work. The compass being talked about works at an intuitive level and develops as we learn from our own experiences and most importantly, from the experiences of others. This book talks about the many facets of leadership like perseverance, self-belief and building effective teams, each serving us an opportunity to reflect and develop our compass.

The author has done a very encouraging job and the

onus now shifts to the reader to extract the most from these nuggets of wisdom and chart out their own course with hopefully an even more evolved compass!

R. Gopalakrishnan

Introduction

The great painter and sculptor Michelangelo has several masterpieces to his credit. Perhaps at the top of that list is *David*, his eighteen-foot-tall statue sculpted in marble in Florence, Italy. Now over 500 years old, this icon of Renaissance sculpture continues to attract—and fascinate—millions of visitors every year, from all over the world. Everyone who sees it goes back impressed by the genius of Michelangelo. But I am not sure if they all also take back the story behind the sculpting of this masterpiece.

The story goes that this mammoth eighteen-foot block of marble had been lying around for several years. In fact, it had been around long before Michelangelo was even born. Some great artists, including Leonardo da Vinci, were invited to create something from that slab of marble. They all looked at it and dismissed it as flawed and worthless. Nothing could come of it, they felt. Several years later, Michelangelo got to work on that 'flawed and worthless' piece of marble, and went on to create a magnificent work of art. Apparently, while he was working on *David*, a little boy went up to Michelangelo and asked him why he was banging away at the rock of marble, and hitting it so hard. 'Young man,' said Michelangelo. 'There's an angel inside that rock. I am just setting him free.'

If you think about it, we are all like that rock of marble. There's genius inside each of us. There's a winner inside, waiting to be unleashed. None of us is flawed, none of us worthless. In most cases, we are just waiting for the right sculptor to come along, chisel away at the rock and set the winner inside free.

The Habit of Winning, the book you now hold in your hands, is a bit like a sculptor's toolkit. It is intended to help free the winner within you—and indeed the winners within all the other people you may be working with. And instead of the usual hammers and chisels, what you have in this toolkit are stories. Tales that will help you chip away at some of the unwanted bits of marble, and unleash the winner within.

There's a leader inside each and every one of us, waiting to emerge and rise to his full potential. Never mind who you are or what you do, it's a good thing to remember that you are a leader too. Everyone is. Some of us might lead small teams of people. Some might lead large organizations. Armies perhaps. Or even countries.

But it is good to remember that each and every one of us leads a life—our own.

And in every case, the quality of the results depends squarely on the leader. As is often seen, the speed of the leader determines the rate of the pack. Also, how good a life can be, depends entirely on the leader. On you. Your life, your successes and failures, the joy and the agony are all because of you, the leader of that life. Makes sense then to ensure that you strive to become the best you can be. You owe it to yourself. And to the world around you. You are not just another piece of marble. You are a masterpiece—waiting to be set free.

A picture may be worth a thousand words, but when it comes to getting your message to register in the minds of people—or indeed in your own—nothing works quite as well as a story. Stories make ideas and concepts come alive and by shifting the action to another world and another time, they help us step back and see things from a whole new perspective. They make the impossible seem possible. And in times of seemingly unending despair, they open a window of hope. They inspire. And best of all, they are memorable. They stick. In our minds. In our heads. In our subconscious.

The Habit of Winning is all about helping that leader inside you come into his own. We all have unlimited potential, and we can all improve. This book will hopefully provide some pointers. It won't change you. Far from it.

It will merely help you become the person you are meant to be. And help you help others to rise to their full potential too.

How do you define a vision for your organization? How do you create a winning team where the sum of the parts is clearly far greater than the whole? What do great leaders do? Why do some people do far more under one leader than under another? How do you keep going in the face of adversity? How do you instil the virtues of patience and perseverance and teamwork?

And how do you find balance in life? How do you set goals and achieve them? How can you be, have and do all the things you always wanted to?

The Habit of Winning is all about bringing out the best in yourself and in the people you work with, about building great teams and winning. It is also about finding balance, being happy, making a difference. To yourself. And to the world around you.

The Habit of Winning is really a collection of stories. Stories that made a difference to my life. And will make to yours too, I hope. I have been lucky, nay privileged, to work with some truly outstanding people. And I have learnt a lot from them. Some of my most vital lessons have been not from bosses but from salesmen and lift operators, accountants and factory folks. Ordinary people and, in almost every case, extraordinary leaders.

So in *The Habit of Winning* you'll find lessons from cola

wars and cricketing heroes. From frogs and fish, and rabbits and sharks. And while you may have heard some of these stories earlier, hopefully they will help ignite a new passion, and a renewed sense of purpose in your mind. And in your team's heads and hearts too. Find yourself stuck in a rut? Feel like throwing in the towel? Hopefully you'll find a story here that helps you get over it and emerge victorious. And if you are trying to lead your team over hurdles and barriers, hopefully you'll find stories that help you get them to keep the faith, and discover strengths they did not know existed within them. If you are trying to communicate with your team, you might find that a story can sometimes be the best way to urge them into action. Stories can be powerful. Quite like the blow of a hammer on a slab of marble. Turn the pages, and you might find a story that resonates with the piece of marble you are working on.

Go ahead, enjoy the journey as you watch the winner inside you emerge and grow. Use these stories to communicate with yourself and your team, and watch them turn into works of art too. And keep adding your own stories to the toolkit. That will make you an even better sculptor.

It would be a pity to have to vanish from the face of this earth with the music still playing inside you. It would be a shame to leave this world with that leader still hidden inside that rock of marble. It would be tragic to have had so many wonderful pieces of marble all around you, all erroneously dismissed as somewhat faulty and worthless. Come on, unleash the leader within.

It has rightly been said that leaders create leaders, not followers. Chisel away, start now. And may a thousand leaders bloom.

Remember, it's never too late to become what you might have been.

I

VISION AND GOALS

Breaking Stones. And Building Monuments

It happened some years ago on a deserted street in Rome. It was a hot, sunny afternoon. A woman was walking down the street, shopping bags in her hands, whistling a tune to herself, when she noticed a group of labourers breaking stones by the roadside. Clack-clack . . . clack-clack . . . they went as their hammers pounded on the stones, splitting them into smaller and smaller bits.

Intrigued, the woman went up to one of the workmen and asked him what he was doing. 'Can't you see?' came the rather terse reply, as the man looked up and wiped the sweat from his brow. 'I am breaking stones.'

Walking a little farther, she saw another man, also breaking stones. 'What are you doing?' she asked him. 'Me?' he replied. 'Oh, I am helping build the world's tallest cathedral!'

Think about it. Apply this analogy to your workplace.

How do your colleagues in the organization perceive their roles? As mere stone breakers, or as the builders of the world's tallest cathedral?

Does your frontline salesperson see his role as just a 'sales rep'? Or does he pride himself on being part of a world-class team that is aiming to be the best in the business? Does the woman in your front office see herself as just a 'receptionist'? Or as the ambassador and the first point of contact of an organization that is aiming to be the best in the business? The difference in the way your frontline members—your 'stone breakers'—think can spell the difference between a terrific organization and an ordinary one. It can mean the difference between achieving your vision or falling short of your targets.

And how do successful leaders ensure that their organizations comprehend and share their vision? How do they get individuals to see their roles clearly as indispensable to a larger, grander plan?

They do that by articulating a vision for the business. By spelling out a dream that the entire organization can identify with and relate to.

They then make sure that every individual understands his role in helping the team realize that vision.

And they also make sure that there is respect in the organization for every individual, for what he brings to the table. For his unique contribution in helping the organization realize its dream.

Thus, every individual focuses not only on delivering the best in his assigned role but also on being a fruitful part of a larger winning team. And he basks in the glory of knowing that in his own way, he makes a difference.

P.M. Sinha (popularly called 'Suman'), former CEO of PepsiCo India, was a master at such vision sharing. He created what he called an upside-down organization. And his favourite slide in any presentation was the organization chart, which showed the frontline salesmen right on top, with the rest of the organization under them, supporting their efforts. The CEO was right at the bottom of that inverted pyramid, his role being to support the entire organization.

There were other practices too that helped foster this culture of togetherness. There were no bosses or 'Sirs'. Suman was called Suman by the entire team. Everyone wore identical shirts to work, with the Pepsi logo emblazoned on the pockets, right across their hearts. In every visit to the market, in every conference, Suman made sure that he projected his frontliners as his heroes. In fact, the Pepsi salesman was immortalized in a popular TV commercial featuring Sachin Tendulkar. Remember the genial sardarji scolding Sachin for smashing a ball into the windshield of his Pepsi truck, and then cooling down to say, 'Oye, relax yaar . . . have a Pepsi!'?

It isn't surprising that Suman succeeded in creating a first-rate sales team, where every salesman and every route agent who drove a Pepsi truck saw himself as a hero, out on a battle, ready to kill the enemy (a.k.a. Coke) and make Pepsi the number one cola in the country. In fact, if you stopped a Pepsi truck and asked the salesman what he was doing, chances were high that he'd say he was helping Pepsi win the cola war. Not just 'selling Pepsi'.

Once, on a visit to the Kennedy Space Center, Florida, to review the progress on his grand vision of putting a man on the moon, charismatic American President John F. Kennedy saw a janitor eyeing him shyly. 'What do you do here?' J.F.K. asked her, to acknowledge her presence and strike up a conversation.

Pushing her hair back with her hand, she replied: 'I am helping America put a man on the moon.'

Indeed, some time after Kennedy 'shared' his dream of putting a man on the moon, Neil Armstrong was taking 'one small step for man, a giant leap for mankind'. And in India, Pepsi took on the world's most valuable brand, and won.

Behind these successes were armies of salesmen and janitors—stone breakers, if you please—who saw themselves as part of a larger mission. They saw themselves as builders of the world's tallest cathedral, as people who were making a difference.

And what a difference that made!

'How do you and your colleagues in the organization perceive your roles? As stone breakers? Or as builders of the world's tallest cathedral?'

Climbing the Mountain

Folks, it's quiz time!

If two people want to climb a mountain together, what's the most important thing they need to get to the top? Is it equipment? Or training? Or teamwork? Or favourable weather conditions?

Well, they need all of these for sure. But the most important thing is the mountain itself. They need a clear goal!

Too often, we get obsessed with the equipment and the training but have no clear goals. The best mountain-climbing equipment is of little use if you don't have a mountain to climb.

We are all very fortunate. We have the most fabulous equipment there is. We have access to training. And there are colleagues out there, waiting to help us succeed. But we need to have our own mountains. Our own goals.

And once you have your own mountain to climb,

everything changes. Magically. You get a sense of purpose. You begin to want to climb that peak. You become disciplined. You get up early, you brave the cold, you watch your diet, you seek out experts, you read the books . . . All because you now have a mountain to climb. A peak to conquer.

So instead of complaining about your equipment or your training, and worrying about buying more sophisticated equipment, set your own goals first.

Find your own mountain. That could be the first step towards transforming your whole life.

Go ahead. Write down your goals. Today.

Get your own mountain. And take the first step towards feeling on top of the world.

The best mountain-climbing equipment is of little use if you don't have a mountain to climb.

Goals: The Secret to Making Your Dreams Come True

True story? Not sure. But the story goes that in 1963, some behavioural scientists performed an experiment with the graduating class of Harvard Business School. They asked the students if they had written down goals for themselves. Their goals for life. For the future. On paper.

A mere 3 per cent of the class had actually written down goals. Yes. Just 3 per cent.

Well, twenty-five years later, the scientists again got in touch with the class of '63. To find out how they had done in their careers. And in their lives.

And guess what?

They found that the net worth of the 3 per cent of the class that had written down goals was MORE than the net worth of the rest of that batch. Not just that; the 3 per cent written-down-goalwallahs seemed to be happier, doing what they wanted and leading far more fulfilling lives.

Incredible. But, I believe, it's true. And it could be true for all of us.

What are your goals? What do you want to achieve? What do you want to be, have, do? In life. At work. In relationships. Whatever it be, write it down. Now. Just write it down. Not later, not tomorrow—now!

And commit yourself to action. Commit yourself to doing what it takes to achieve your goals. Take action. Make sure that everything you do is taking you closer to your goals. (If it isn't, don't do it.)

And finally, take a step today. However small it may be, but take that first step today. If you want to lose weight, walk that 45-minute walk—today! If you want to be the best salesperson, make that extra sales call—today!

You'll see the difference. As the Nike guys would say, just do it.

It takes just three steps.

Step one: Write down your goals.

Step two: Make a commitment to action, to doing what it takes.

Step three: Take the first step. Today!

Come on, make a beginning. You owe it to yourself. And you have nothing to lose.

What are your goals? What do you want to be, have, do? Whatever it be, write it down.

Don't Change Your Rabbit!

The power of Focus. The power of Persistence. I believe these are powerful ingredients of success, but just how powerful they are was brilliantly brought to life on a memorable trip to China.

In an auditorium packed to the gills with young Chinese entrepreneurs (mostly of the online variety), I had the privilege of listening to Jack Ma, the charismatic founder of the world's largest B2B portal, alibaba.com.

Jack used to be an English teacher in Beijing. His proficiency in the language meant that he was much in demand when trade delegations came into mainland China or when groups of Chinese businessmen went over to the US to seek trade opportunities. Jack saw, first hand, two phenomena at work.

One, the Chinese businessmen—despite their ignorance of the English language—had a lot to offer and seemed capable of taking on the world. Two, the emerging medium of the Internet seemed to hold the potential to take China to the world like nothing else could. Putting the two together, Jack roped in eighteen friends who shared his vision. And thus was born alibaba.com, in Jack's apartment in Hangzhou.

He rode the initial euphoria. He survived the bust. And, along the way, alibaba.com gobbled up Yahoo in China. Now, Jack presides over a hugely successful business. When Alibaba went public in 2007, it was a spectacular debut on the Hong Kong Stock Exchange and the initial public offering was the second largest for any Internet company in the world—behind only Google's.

What's Jack's advice to budding Internet entrepreneurs? What's his formula for success? Like the man himself, his advice too is simple. 'Believe in your dream and believe in yourself. Do it because you want to do it, not because the investor wants you to do it, not because other people want you to do it. Don't give up the dream. Do whatever you can to make sure you are getting close to your dream every day. Find good people, get your customers to love you and stick to that. Learn quickly, and learn from others the tactics and the skills, but don't change your dream.' Don't change your dream!

Jack then illustrated the power of focus. 'In 2000, I said that if there are nine rabbits running around and you want to catch one, focus only on one. If you try to catch them all, you may end up with none. If the rabbit you're chasing proves elusive, change your tactics but don't change the rabbit. Just stick to it. There are so many opportunities, you cannot catch all of them. Get one first, put it in your pocket, then catch the others.'

Powerful advice that. Often, we are guilty of getting tempted by multiple opportunities, and in trying to grab them all, we end up with nothing. The first challenge for most of us lies in not choosing which rabbit to catch. Setting clear goals is the key to starting on the journey to success. Next, we get distracted by other rabbits hopping about and lose our focus. Think of all the diversifications that made robust corporates shift focus from their core strengths to flirt with new ideas, which led to their under-performance.

If you lived in Gujarat in the 1980s, you would have grown up savouring the unique flavours of Vadilal ice cream. You could have sworn it was the world's best ice cream—capable of becoming the biggest and the best ice cream brand in the world. Did Vadilal get there? Well, not quite. Along the way, Vadilal saw that processed, ready-to-eat foods would be a big category in India. Good insight. So they got in there, and chased that rabbit. Then with the dawn of liberalization in India, they figured that dealing in forex could be a big business idea. So they chased that rabbit too. Then real estate, a booming sector. That was rabbit number four. And then chemicals . . . Vadilal just chased too many rabbits for their own good.

(Vadilal ice creams are still very yummy, and the business, still rather small.)

Even when we focus on one rabbit, our inability to catch it pushes us quickly—too quickly sometimes—to chase other rabbits. We lack persistence. We give up too soon. When I see bright young people quit jobs in a jiffy because they aren't climbing the ladder quickly enough, it makes me cry. I wish they knew and heeded Jack's words: 'Change tactics. Don't change the rabbit.'

As I watched Jack on stage—consummate showman, local hero, global leader—speaking extempore to the massive audience, I too was awed. Then, I saw something else that made a huge impact. Two seats away from me was a young lad (never quite figured why, but Chinese tend to look younger than their age) hanging on to every word of Jack's, scribbling every little nugget, making copious notes. Don't see that too often in any gathering elsewhere in the world.

The world better watch out! With their native intelligence, their willingness to learn, their ability to slog, their determination to succeed—and with leaders like Jack showing the way—China's businessmen look set to conquer the world.

They know which rabbit they want to catch. Do you?

Identify the rabbit you want to catch, and focus only on that one. If you try and catch them all, you may end up with none. If the rabbit proves elusive, change your tactics but don't change the rabbit.

II

SELF-BELIEF

Károly Takács and the Winner's Mindset

The next time you watch your favourite sport on TV, or read about the stars of the game, it might be a good idea to participate in a little sport yourself. Try this. Get inside the minds of the sportsmen. Get into their shoes. Take a peek inside the psyches of all those sporting heroes. The record breakers as well as the favourites who lose out. Also the person who drops a catch or misses a penalty. And the sportsman who perhaps missed out due to an unfortunate injury, and is watching the game on TV at home. Think of what must be going through their minds. This could be a fascinating game.

Sport is a terrific metaphor for life, and there are several sporting stories that inspire and motivate us. But perhaps none more so than the tale of Károly Takács. You may not have heard of him, but his life story is worth a listen.

Károly was a sergeant in the Hungarian army. In 1938, the twenty-eight-year-old was the country's top pistol shooter, having won most major national and international championships. He was—by a mile—the favourite to win gold at the 1940 Tokyo Olympic Games.

Then, disaster struck.

At an army training session, a hand grenade accidentally exploded in Károly's hand. And blew it away. His shooting hand. Not only did his entire Olympic dream crash, he also lost a limb.

'Why me?' Károly could have been excused for asking the question most of us would have asked. You would understand it too if he wallowed in self-pity, an understandable reaction for someone after such a tragic turn of events. You would sympathize with him if he were to become a recluse, a living example of how fate can devastate the best-laid plans.

Oh no, not Károly. He was made of sterner stuff.

Instead of focusing on what he had lost—his right hand, his potentially gold medal-winning shooting hand—he chose to focus on what he still had. He had mental strength, the mindset of a winner, the determination to succeed and yes, a healthy left hand. A left hand which, he thought, he could train and transform into the world's best shooting hand.

After a month in hospital, Károly went out and, away from the glare of the world, began practising to shoot with his left hand. Despite the pain his body still reeled under, despite the strain the left hand had to undergo to also do all that the right hand had earlier done, he stayed focused on his goal: to make his left hand the best shooting hand in the world.

One year later, Károly resurfaced at the national shooting championship in Hungary. His colleagues were delighted to see him. They complimented him on his courage, and his fabulous gesture of coming over to see them shoot. But they were taken aback when Károly told them that he wasn't there to see them shoot; he was there to compete with them.

And compete he did. In fact, Károly won the championship. Just one year after losing his right hand. He won with his left hand.

Károly's decision to practise quietly, away from scrutiny, was significant. It is easy for people to ridicule you for dreaming big. It is also very easy for you to stay afloat in your misery for a sympathy wave laps at you from all over.

Unfortunately for Károly, his Olympic dream remained unrealized for a while, as two successive Games were cancelled due to the world war.

In 1948, the Olympics came to London. Károly was chosen to represent Hungary in the pistol shooting event. And he won gold. Shooting with his left hand.

Imagine being a gold medal favourite, losing your

shooting hand in an accident, yet picking yourself up from the shattered mess, training your left hand to shoot as well or better, and going on to win the Olympic gold.

Four years later. Helsinki Olympics. Pistol shooting event. Who won gold? No surprises here. Károly Takács.

That is the stuff champions are made of.

We all have moments in our lives when we seem so close to glory but suddenly lose everything. When it seems that the world is conspiring to destroy us. Our dreams get shattered. We feel vanquished. Crushed. Beaten. Defeated. And we cry aloud, 'Why me?'

When that happens, think of Károly. In fact, think like him. Don't worry about what you've lost. Focus on what you still have. Your inner strength. Your mental toughness. No one can take these away.

Don't lose yourself to self-pity. Pick yourself up quickly. Momentum is key. Károly was back on the practice range a month after the accident. When you are down, think like a boxer: if you are knocked down, you need to stand up in ten seconds or less. One extra second, and it's all over.

Set yourself a goal and focus on achieving it. A goal helps channelize the mind and body to work on what needs to be achieved, rather than looking back and worrying about past losses, about what might have been. When your mind is flooded with negative thoughts, it's not easy to wish them away. You need a positive thought—a goal—to replace and banish negative thoughts.

Winning a gold medal in pistol shooting is less about the hand, more about the mind. Life's like that. Winning is less about skills, more about attitude. Skills can be acquired, as Károly demonstrated with his left hand.

When you watch the next game of cricket or football, when you see the winners there, remember to win something for yourself too.

Remember the Károly Takács mindset. The winner's mindset!

We all have moments in our lives when we seem so close to glory but suddenly lose everything. When that happens, don't worry about what you've lost. Focus on what you still have.

Break Your Mental Barriers: The Roger Bannister Story

If you think you can, you can. If you think you can't, you are right!

To understand the truth in that dictum, let's journey back to the 1950s.

In the world of athletics then, it was widely believed that no human could run the mile in less than four minutes. The best time was credited to Sweden's Gunder Haegg, who ran the mile in 4 minutes and 1.4 seconds. And he did that in 1945. The record stood for several years, and doctors and athletes and sports experts were unanimous in the view that the four-minute barrier could not be broken. Not possible, they said. Can't be done. In fact, it was believed that no man could attempt it without causing significant physical harm to his body.

Then, on 6 May 1954, Roger Bannister did the impossible. At a track and field event in London, Roger ran the mile and touched the finishing line in 3 minutes and 59.4 seconds, thereby shattering the four-minute barrier. He did what they had said was impossible. His body did what they said no body could.

John Landy—an accomplished runner and Roger's rival—had a personal best time of 4 minutes and 1.5 seconds till then. In fact, after running the mile in under 4 minutes and 2 seconds three times, John said that the four-minute barrier was 'like a wall'—it couldn't be broken. However, just fifty-six days after Roger smashed the four-minute-mile mental barrier, John too broke his own mental wall and ran the mile in 3 minutes and 57.9 seconds.

That's not all. By the end of 1957, sixteen other runners had run the mile in less than four minutes. The mental barrier had been well and truly smashed!

So what actually happened? Did the athletes' bodies suddenly get stronger? Was there new technology to improve the runners' shoes? Did training methods get enhanced? Did athletes simply try harder? None of the above, really. It's just that the mental barrier—the self-limiting belief that a mile can't be run in under four minutes—was shattered. And that opened up the floodgates.

Roger was a doctor by training. And as he explained later, to him it seemed illogical that you could run a mile in four minutes and a bit, but could not break four minutes. His mind refused to accept that barrier. In reality, what Roger did was prove that the barrier was not a physiological one—it was merely a mental barrier. What Roger did on that windy day was not merely set a new world record; he, in fact, demonstrated that breaking mental barriers can help us deliver breakthrough performances.

We are all like that. We all have our beliefs about what we can achieve, and what we can't. And our success is limited by those barriers. Even our effort is often restricted by those barriers. We don't try, because we see those barriers. What Robin Sharma calls 'those little invisible fences'.

As the Roger Bannister story shows, once he broke the four-minute-mile barrier, the mental barrier in the minds of all runners was shattered. And soon thereafter, sixteen people ran the mile in under four minutes.

Life is all about breaking mental barriers. Leaping across and clean over those little invisible fences. Dreaming the impossible dream.

What's your four-minute barrier? What's holding you and your team back? Go on, shatter that barrier. Today.

If you think you can, you can. If you think you can't, you are right!

Acres of Diamonds

'Acres of Diamonds' was the title of a talk delivered by Russell Conwell in the early part of the twentieth century. Russell was an American Baptist, orator and founder of the Temple University in Philadelphia. His talk became so popular that Russell is reported to have delivered it over 6000 times around the world. At the heart of the talk is a little story—about acres of diamonds—as relevant today as it was a hundred years ago.

The story goes that many years ago there was this prosperous Persian farmer named Al Hafed. He had a large tract of land, and an even larger heart. He would play host to visiting traders, travelling salesmen and explorers and priests, and it was from one such priest that he learnt about diamonds. Diamonds that could make people rich, and make all their dreams come true.

Sensing an opportunity to earn a fortune, Al Hafed decided to go out and hunt for the diamonds. 'I want them, and I am going to go look for them,' he told the priest. He sold his farm, left his family in the care of neighbours and went looking for diamonds. Unfortunately, even after spending six months—and a lot of money—he did not meet with any success. Broke and heartbroken, he died soon after.

Meanwhile, back on the land Al Hafed had sold, the new owner was watering the plants one evening, when he suddenly saw something glistening. It was a large stone and, seeing its radiance, he picked it up and put it on his mantelpiece at home. That night, the old priest happened to stop by. Seeing the large stone, he exclaimed: 'Ah, a diamond! Is Al Hafed back?' 'No,' said the new owner, 'I just picked it up from the garden. In fact, there are lots of such stones all over the garden!'

Yes, there were literally acres of diamonds in the plot of land which Al Hafed had sold and gone away from, in his search for diamonds. It's an old story but the lessons are as valid today. For individuals and organizations. The goals we seek, the wealth we lust for, they are all there—right beneath our feet. Often in our quest for more, we believe we need to abandon our current position and go out looking for success. We think a change of job or a change of industry or even a change of location is essential for success.

Why do we fail to recognize the diamonds in our own backyard, under our own feet? That's probably because diamonds often appear in their rough, uncut form. And polishing those uncut stones is hard work. Very hard work in most cases. Like diamonds in their rough form, we fail to recognize the opportunities that come our way, because opportunities often come disguised as hard work.

Large corporations too are guilty of ignoring their acres of diamonds. Starved for growth they think they've hit a wall, and go into unrelated diversifications, exposing their traditional areas of strength. Only to find a newcomer come in and mint a fortune—in a market considered non-existent by the leader.

Good lesson to remember, in times good and bad. We all have acres of diamonds right beneath our feet. We only need to learn to look!

Often, in our quest for more, we believe we need to abandon our current position and go out looking for success. We fail to recognize the diamonds lying right under our feet.

Tyrone Bogues: Standing Tall!

It probably won't surprise you to find out that the average height of an NBA basketball player is 6′7″. It's a sport that clearly demands and rewards tall men. Look at some of the all-time greats: Michael Jordan (6′2″), Kobe Bryant (6′6″), Magic Johnson (6′9″), Kareem Abdul-Jabbar (7′2″), Yao Ming, the Chinese sensation (7′6″). Each of them has a huge fan following and they have all entertained and inspired millions of young people around the world.

While you are probably aware of the exploits of most of these stars, have you heard of Tyrone 'Muggsy' Bogues?

Tyrone was an NBA star too. In a career spanning sixteen seasons, Tyrone was one of NBA's all-time leaders in assist-to-turnover ratios. Voted as Charlotte Hornets' Most Valuable Player for several years, Tyrone also held the team record for maximum minutes played, steals, assists and turnovers. Quite an achievement that!

But here's what really made Tyrone a crowd favourite and an all-time hero. In a world dominated by the tall men who could easily rest their elbows on the hoop, Tyrone was a short guy. In fact, at 5′3″, Bogues was—and still remains—the shortest player in NBA history.

As a child growing up in the bylanes of Baltimore, Tyrone practised the slam dunk by standing on upturned milk crates. He was short and, though he was passionate about the sport, no one really thought he could ever be NBA material. After all, he was so short! But Tyrone was determined to succeed, and ignored naysayers and sceptics. What he lacked in height, he made up with his speed, stamina and explosiveness on court. 'I always believed in myself,' he said in an interview with *Sports Illustrated*. 'That's the type of attitude I always took out on the floor, knowing that I belonged; that with my talents, my abilities, there's a place for me out there.'

Tyrone became a terrific symbol of determination, hard work and self-belief. And he demonstrated how by ignoring your critics, focusing on your strengths and not getting caught up in your limitations, you can achieve your goals. 'You can't dwell on what people think you can't do,' he once famously remarked.

Think about it. How often do we allow the world around us to decide whether we are good enough? 'You can't do this because . . .' is a refrain we hear all the time. And we let our goals slip away because we think we are not tall enough, or rich enough, or educated enough . . . Pick your favourite self-limiting belief!

There are several lessons to be learnt from the life and times of Tyrone Bogues. Focus on your strengths. And not on your weaknesses. Ignore the pessimists and non-believers. Don't waste time trying to set right limitations.

Organizations and individuals can benefit from the Tyrone mindset. Think of the detergents markets in the late 1970s. Unilever and Procter & Gamble were the dominant players worldwide, and it was well established that brand-building skills, marketing wizardry and huge advertising budgets were prerequisites to success. Quite like being a six-footer was seen as essential to success in basketball.

Then a local Gujarati businessman with some familiarity with chemicals and detergents decided to sell a washing powder. He'd make some of it in his backyard, load it on to his bicycle and sell it in the neighbourhood. No brand-building skills, no hot-shot MBAs, zero advertising. But by focusing on his core strength—which was low cost—Karsanbhai Patel managed to create the Nirma phenomenon, which took on multinational superpowers with considerable success.

For most of us, the temptation is to focus on our weaknesses and ignore our strengths. When a ten-year-old is fond of reading and can bowl a cricket ball reasonably quick but is weak at mathematics, what do we do? We send him to maths tuition, not to a class for writing skills or cricket coaching sessions. Why?

There's a Tyrone inside each of us, struggling to become an NBA great. But we are busy giving him vitamin tonics and stretching his limbs, trying to make him taller. And not allowing him to show his speed and dexterity. There's a Nirma-like success story waiting to happen in our businesses. But we are busy raising money, getting sexy advertising, hiring marketing talent, instead of capitalizing on our unique low-cost proposition.

Go on, unleash the Tyrone magic inside you. Forget your limitations. Ignore the pessimists. Build on your unique strengths.

Success is beckoning. Are you ready?

Focus on your strengths. And not on your weaknesses. Don't waste time trying to set right the limitations.

The Water Bearer, the Cracked Pot

Come examination time, and the city pages of newspapers get filled with stories of examination fever gripping the city. The agony of misplaced hall tickets, anxious parents rushing their children to test centres through traffic snarls, valiant stories of injured kids taking their exams . . .

If you've been reading carefully, you will know another set of stories springing up along with the exams. Stories of children taking their own lives, for fear of failure. Now that's a real tragedy. A tragedy that underscores the misplaced emphasis our society has placed on examination grades. The sad tale of people being branded failures for life, merely because of their inability to score 35 per cent marks in a test paper. When will we learn?

The tale of the water bearer comes to my mind. Every morning he would carry two pots of water tied at either end of a pole resting on his shoulder. One pot was perfect, the other was cracked. By the time he reached his master's house, the perfect pot would still be full but the cracked pot would be half empty, having leaked some of the water along the way.

This went on for a while. Every morning, the water bearer would reach his master's house with one and a half pots of water. The perfect pot felt proud of his accomplishment, of doing what was expected of him. The cracked pot felt bad, guilty of letting down the poor water bearer and delivering only half the water. 'I am ashamed,' said the pot to the bearer. 'I let you down, every day. I only deliver half the amount of water I should. Why don't you just smash me to pieces?'

'Oh, you shouldn't really feel so bad,' said the kind bearer. 'When we go to the master's house today, take a look at the beautiful flowers along the path. I am sure they will make you feel better.'

Sure enough, the cracked pot saw the bed of flowers along the path, dancing in the breeze. It cheered him but only a bit, because as they neared the master's house, he realized he had yet again delivered only half the water. 'I am sorry, I am letting you down!' he said with a sigh.

'Oh no!' said the water bearer. 'Didn't you notice that all the flowers were only on your side of the path? That's because I noticed the crack and took advantage of it. I planted the flower seeds on your side of the path and you watered them every day. Without you, we wouldn't have those beautiful flowers!'

What is true of pots is true of people too. We all have our cracks and flaws, and the real challenge is to find good use for our unique talents.

Think of a little boy with a polio-affected arm . . . What chance do you think he would have of playing a competitive sport like cricket? Well, B.S. Chandrasekhar did just that. He used that polio-affected arm to his advantage, turning the wrist like few could, to bowl those googlies and flippers that set up many a famous Test victory, making him one of India's all-time great bowlers.

Think of the scientist called Dr Spencer Silver, who worked to create a new glue. Something went wrong with the molecular structure. The glue would stick but not quite, so you could pull it off. A failure? Hardly, when you consider that it led to the invention of the ubiquitous Post-its!

Those flaws, those cracks, they probably hide the magic within. That little boy flunking his maths examination may just be a Sachin Tendulkar. That young boy struggling to get past Class 10 may just be a certain Dhirubhai Ambani. Let's not condemn the cracked pots. Let's work harder ourselves to discover those talents and find uses for their special abilities.

Failing to do that probably means that there is a real crack. Not in the pot but in the beholder.

We all have our cracks and flaws. The challenge is to find good use for our unique talents.

Good Ol' Charlie Brown and the Uthappa Factor

The difference between successful people and failures is rather simple. Those who succeed recall past successes and wins. And those who fail remember only misses and failures. And, as is often said, it's all in the mind.

Flashback to 5 September 2007. The sixth One-day International cricket match between England and India at the Oval. England, leading the series 3–2, batted first and put up an impressive 316 in 50 overs. India, at the start of the fiftieth over, were 307 for 8, with Robin Uthappa and Ramesh Powar at the crease. 10 runs to win, 2 wickets in hand.

Two singles off the first two balls meant India still had to make 8 to win off 4 balls. And that's when Robin played an audacious-looking stroke that saw him transform instantly from a raw twenty-year-old kid into a man. A shot that is probably still etched in your mind if you watched that game. Playing his first international series, Robin shuffled across outside his off stump and scooped a straight ball perfectly pitched on his middle stump, hoisting it over the wicketkeeper's head towards fine leg for 4. Next ball, another 4, and the game was won.

That scoop shot was a stroke of supreme confidence, perfectly executed, that took India to the doorstep of victory. But had Robin missed that ball, his stumps would have been knocked over. It would have looked ugly, even embarrassing. Experts would have pilloried him for not caring for the team's interest, for playing irresponsibly. For losing India a game. It's a different story that it worked, and Robin's 47 runs off 33 balls meant that India had found a new batting hero.

In the post-match interview, Harsha Bhogle asked Robin about that shot. 'When you played that shot, did it occur to you that if you missed, the critics would have been out baying for your blood? Did the thought of failure ever cross your mind?'

Robin explained that it was a shot that he and the team had been practising in the nets and working on in the build-up to the series. He had got it right several times in the nets, he said. And then those magical words: 'I never thought I'd miss!'

I never thought I'd miss. Wow! And he sure didn't.

Often, too often perhaps, the fear of failure holds us back. As a result, we don't even attempt to do what we are capable of. The thought of failure crowds our minds. We think of the miss. We think of our weaknesses, our limitations. The consequences of failure. The humiliation. The agony of defeat.

And our thoughts become our reality.

Winners think differently. They think of how they've succeeded in the past. Their strengths. They visualize success. They imagine the joy of winning. The glory. The accolades. And bingo—success is theirs.

In that moment of challenge, you can either think of your past successes, or of your failures. The choice is yours. And you impact your outcomes. 'If you think you can, you can. If you think you can't, you are right.'

Do you remember the *Peanuts* comic strips and good ol' Charlie Brown? My personal favourite in that series is a conversation between Lucy and Charlie. As they look out of a window, Lucy exclaims, 'Oh, I see birds and trees, and flowers and sunshine.' And Charlie says, 'I see fingerprints and bugs and smudges.' Lucy tells him, 'Charlie Brown, don't you know that windows are for looking through, not at!'

Our lives are like windows. We can look through our challenges and see the glory and feel the joy of winning. Or we can focus on what is wrong and all we see are our weaknesses and the bugs, the smudges, the difficulties. So when you stand by the window of your life's challenges, choose to look at your strengths. Visualize the joy of winning. Don't focus on your limitations. Don't look at the fingerprints and the smudges.

Learn to be a Robin. Don't think you'll miss. And you won't!

Windows are for looking through, not at! Our lives are like windows. We can look through our challenges and see the glory and feel the joy of winning. Or we can focus on what is wrong and see all our weaknesses.

III

PERSEVERANCE

'Main Khelega!'

The Making of a Champion Called Sachin Tendulkar

24 February 2010: An entire nation erupted with joy as Sachin Tendulkar became the first cricketer to score a double century in a One-day International. In 2961 previous games in international cricket, no man had been able to go on to the 200-run mark. And it was only fitting that the man with the highest number of runs in Test and One-day cricket (and the highest number of centuries in both forms of the game) had achieved the feat.

As newspapers filled column space with stories and vignettes chronicling the life of India's greatest cricketer, I thought about my favourite Sachin story. It's a story that Navjot Singh Sidhu, former Indian cricketer-turned-politician, loves to tell. While the world rises to salute a truly outstanding cricketer, this little tale probably explains, in some small measure, the making of a genius. A giant among men. The Little Legend!

December 1989, Sialkot, Pakistan. It was the fourth Test match of the India–Pakistan series. And, as it happens, just the fourth Test of Sachin's career.

Making his debut at sixteen, the cherub-faced, fuzzy-haired Sachin had already won admirers, being widely seen as a precocious talent. However, several young stars had sparkled briefly in India's cricketing firmament and then, almost as suddenly, faded away—a gross injustice to their enormous talents. Let down on the long highway to success by a faltering mental make-up, that didn't quite back up their reserves of talent. Would Sachin go the same way? Was he being blooded too early for his own good?

The series was level 0–0 after three Tests. Despite conceding a first innings lead of 65 in the fourth Test, Pakistan hit back strongly through blistering spells from Waqar Younis and Wasim Akram, reducing India to 38 runs for 4 wickets in their second innings. India was suddenly staring at defeat, with which they would lose the series too.

In walked Sachin to join Sidhu. Experienced pros like Sanjay Manjrekar and Kris Srikkanth, Mohammed Azharuddin and Ravi Shastri had found the Pak attack too hot to handle and were back in the pavilion. How would the new kid on the block cope?

Waqar bowled a nasty bouncer that went smack on Sachin's nose. The poor boy was badly hit and his nose began to bleed profusely. It made for a sad sight on TV, and most women watching were convinced that there ought to be a law to prevent a sixteen-year-old from being subjected to such brutality.

As the Indian team physiotherapist rushed to offer first-aid and the Pakistanis gathered to check out the bloody sight, Sidhu recalls walking down to a shaken—and still bleeding—Sachin. As the physio tried to stop the bleeding, Sidhu suggested to Sachin that he should retire hurt and come out later. That would give him time to get his nose fixed, regain his composure and hopefully return to a less menacing attack. 'Go take a break,' said Sidhu. He feared this might just be the end of another promising career.

'Come in, I'll attend to you,' said the helpful physio.

But Sachin brushed them away, almost annoyed that they should even suggest that he walk away. '*Main khelega!*' he said. 'I'll play.' And, in that moment, says Sidhu, a star was born. Those two words verbalized the fierce determination of a young man who wasn't going to quit.

Sachin could have gone into the relative comfort of the dressing room but he didn't. People watching would have understood but he knew his heart wouldn't understand. The heat was on. India was in trouble. The pace attack had its tail up. The blood was staining his gloves, his shirt, his face, his spirit.

But the kid would have none of it. *Main khelega* it was. Sachin went on to score 57 runs and shared in the match-saving 101-run partnership with Sidhu. With two words—*main khelega*—talent transformed into genius, that day in Sialkot.

It's always like that. What separates champions from mere mortals is not just talent. It's attitude. It's mental strength. It's the willingness to fight when the chips are down. It's the *main khelega* spirit. The spirit that puts the team's need ahead of one's own interest. *Main khelega* says it's not just about me, it's about my team.

There are times in our lives when the pressure mounts and we feel like throwing in the towel and calling it quits. That's just the time when you need to put your hand up and be counted. Time to say *main khelega*.

As a leader, you may often feel that the world is conspiring to knock you down. You may be looking to win but defeat stares you in the face. At times like these, all a leader looks for is a few good men in his team. For people who say *main khelega*. And this spirit is contagious. As one man puts his hand up, another hand goes up. And another. And a team starts believing in itself. In its ability to fight, and win.

Over the last two decades, Sachin has entertained us with his performances. We've watched with awe as he's pulled off incredible wins. And we've watched with anguish when he's failed—and with him have crashed an entire nation's hopes. He has helped us live our dreams, helped us win. In his own way, he's helped us feel good about ourselves. Made us proud to be Indians.

But perhaps Sachin's biggest contribution is teaching an entire nation to stand up and fight. To learn never to give up. To say *main khelega*.

Some years down, long after the little master blaster has hung up his boots, when we tell our grandchildren about the exploits of a batting legend, we should remember to tell them—and teach them—those two magic words that defined the spirit of the champion, and translated talent into performance.

Thanks, Sachin, for the entertainment. Thanks for all those wins. And yes, thanks for showing us the virtues of the *main khelega* spirit.

There will be times when the pressure mounts and you feel like throwing in the towel and calling it quits. That's just the time when you need to put up your hand and be counted. Time to say *main khelega*. I'll play. What separates champions from mere mortals is not just talent. It's attitude. It's mental strength.

The Chinese Bamboo

My favourite spot at home—and my wife's pride and joy—is a little palm-and-bamboo garden she's managed to create in the balcony of our apartment. So every morning, that's where we sit and devour the day's newspapers, with some freshly brewed south Indian filter coffee making the news seem just a wee bit more interesting!

And it's probably this new patch of green that sparked off my interest in the Chinese bamboo. A tree that grows really tall—to a height of over eighty feet. It takes around five years and three months to grow to its full height. But here's the interesting bit. For the first five years after you plant the seed, you see nothing. Absolutely nothing. Except perhaps a little shoot springing out of the bulb and struggling to make a squiggle.

And then, in the next ninety days, it shoots up to a towering eighty feet.

Can you believe it? For the first sixty months, all the growth is invisible, below the surface. The Chinese bamboo's roots create a complex network, like a miniature version of the London Underground. It is these strong roots that, when fully developed, help support a tree that will soar above all else.

And in the next ninety days—yes, merely ninety days—it literally takes off. And becomes as tall as an eight-storeyed building.

In this era of instant coffee and fast food, of get-rich-quick schemes and lose-weight-quicker regimens, of quarterly earnings and month-on-month growth, perhaps we all need to pause and take a lesson from the Chinese bamboo.

Patience has its reward. Nothing of substance happens in a jiffy. All too often, we are unwilling to wait for the pay-off, and tend to settle for shorter trees.

Having sown the seed and having initiated something, when we don't see results, we get impatient. We keep pulling out the sapling to check if the roots are growing. (Well, when you do that, they don't!)

As leaders and bosses, we tend to be impatient for results. And often, too often, we rush to reward the mushrooms that spring up after one spectacular rainy night (and wither away soon after)—only because we can see them! Long-term, sustainable successes take time, and a good question to ask yourself is whether your leadership style encourages—or even allows—the growth of the Chinese bamboo. Or are you creating an organization of stunted, but quickly visible trees?

Every major achievement is almost always preceded by years of toil, hard work, failure, stress, tests of character, determination, sleepless nights . . . All of which help form the network of roots that can then support real accomplishments. And eighty-feet-tall trees.

So the next time you feel frustrated by lack of results and want to give up, don't. Think of the Chinese bamboo.

When you feel the world is unjust and is refusing to recognize your hard work and your commitment, don't panic. Five years of subterranean activity will almost always be followed by three months of meteoric rise.

And ah, yes, after years of slogging it out in relative obscurity, when you finally achieve success, be prepared for people to say: 'Oh, he's so lucky. He's become an overnight success!'

If only they knew about the Chinese bamboo!

Patience has its reward. Nothing of substance happens in a jiffy.

Perseverance and a Man Called Atapattu

Persistence pays. In life, in sport, in your career.

Winston Churchill once visited a school, where the kids asked him what he thought was the secret of success in life. His reply: 'Just seven words . . .' Then, the classic Churchill pause. Then: 'Never give up. Never, never give up!'

Often, too often, we do all the hard work and when we are perhaps just a step away from success, we walk away. Trouble is, we seldom know that we are only a step away. Just a step away from realizing our dreams.

Turning away to choose a new path seems the more attractive option. Without the obvious fear of failure. The grass on the other side looks greener. And we rationalize our failures—bad luck, bad boss, bad karma, bad timing . . . Or all of the above.

Which is why I just love this story of Marvan Atapattu,

the Sri Lankan cricketer. It's a story that Harsha Bhogle, India's most loved cricket commentator, loves to tell, over and over again. Making his debut in Test cricket for Sri Lanka, Marvan scored a duck in his first innings. And again, in his second innings.

They dropped him. So he went back to the nets for more practice. More first-class cricket. More runs. Waiting for that elusive call. And after twenty-one months, he got a second chance.

This time, he tried harder. His scores: 0 in the first innings, 1 in the second. Dropped again, he went back to the grind. And scored tonnes of runs in first-class cricket. Runs that seemed inadequate to erase the painful memories of the Test failures. Well, seventeen months later, opportunity knocked yet again. Marvan got to bat in both innings of the Test. His scores: 0 and 0. Phew!

Back to the grind. Would the selectors ever give him another chance? They said he lacked big-match temperament. His technique wasn't good enough at the highest level. Undaunted, Marvan kept trying.

Three years later, he got another chance. This time, he made runs. He came good. And in an illustrious career thereafter, Marvan went on to score over 5000 runs for Sri Lanka. That included sixteen centuries and six double hundreds. And he went on to captain his country. All this, despite taking over six years to score his second run in Test cricket. Wow! What a guy!

How many of us can handle failure as well as he did? Six years of trying, and failing. He must have been tempted to pursue another career. Change his sport perhaps. Play county cricket. Or, oh well, just give up.

But he didn't. And that made the difference.

We all hear stories of talented people who gave up before their potential was realized. People who changed jobs and careers when success seemed elusive.

The next time you are staring at possible failure or rejection, think of Marvan. And remember this: If you don't give up, if you believe in yourself, if you stay the course, the runs will eventually come. What's more, you could even become captain some day.

Never give up. Never, never give up!

The Anil Kumble Spirit

When Anil Kumble, India's former cricket captain and all-time highest wicket taker, bid adieu to Test cricket, the entire nation seemed to stand up and salute one of India's finest soldiers. A man who rolled his arm over tirelessly to bowl India to many famous wins. And more important, a man who put his hand up every time there was a challenge and a fighter was called for.

Anil Kumble was special. When he made his debut, he looked an unlikely hero. Many wondered what this rather studious-looking, bespectacled mechanical engineer was doing on the cricket field. And in an era of brash, talkative, in-your-face combative cricketers, the stoically quiet Anil could hardly be branded a fighter. But a fighter he was. Fiercely competitive. Learning, all the time. Keeping alive the spirit of the game, always. And oh, desperately, desperately seeking to win.

TV channels and newspaper columns were full of Anil

in the aftermath of his retirement. Which is only fair. After all, there were several highlights in his distinguished eighteen-year career that we could recount, replay and rejoice over. In all that euphoria, guess which was the most cited instance of Anil's greatness?

Was it the fact that he became India's highest ever wicket taker with 619 wickets in Test cricket? Or that he tirelessly bowled over 40,000 balls in Test matches and took 4 wickets or more in an innings sixty-six times? Or was it that magical spell at Kotla against Pakistan, when he took all 10 wickets in an innings? A feat so special, they even named a junction in Bangalore after him! Or were the experts celebrating the two things Kumble did that the other great leg-spinner, Shane Warne, desperately wanted to but couldn't: Score a Test ton, and lead his country! Or was the high point of Anil's career his outstanding statesmanship as a leader in Australia during the Sydney Test fiasco? Anil clearly wore his India cap with pride. And the captain's blazer with quiet dignity.

Significantly, the single most recalled event from his career was Anil coming out to bowl with a fractured jaw, in the Antigua Test against the West Indies.

That was special. Truly special.

To understand its significance, let's flashback to St John's, Antigua, 12 May 2002. It was the fourth Test of the series. A game in which five batsmen had scored a hundred. And yet the most memorable image of the game was of Anil coming on to bowl with a heavily bandaged, fractured jaw.

Batting earlier in the game, Anil was hit on the face by a snorter from Merv Dillon. Despite the nasty blow—which had him spitting blood—Anil soldiered on and batted for four more overs. He was later rushed to hospital, where an X-ray confirmed a fractured jaw. Bad news. He was out of the match, out of the rest of the series, and scheduled to fly back to India the next day.

India made over 500 runs before declaring their first innings. But they were clearly missing their star spinner when the Windies came out to bat. After 45 overs, the Windies were 123 for 2 with Brian Lara at the crease, when—surprise, surprise!—Anil decided to get on to the field and bowl. Fractured jaw, bandage and all. Despite the pain, Anil bowled 14 overs unchanged. And got Brian.

Viv Richards said it was one of the bravest things he had ever seen on a cricket field. 'Cricket has a way of producing inspiring tales of valour, and this one ranks right at the top,' agreed Sunny Gavaskar. And all Anil said was: 'I can now go home with the thought that I tried my best.'

That moment, perhaps better than anything else, defined the greatness of Anil Kumble. A man who could be counted on to give a 100 per cent for his team, for his country, at all times. What makes you a hero is not just the number of wickets you take or the runs you score. It's your willingness to play for your team. To sacrifice personal interest for the larger good. Your willingness to endure personal pain for public good.

In our lives and our careers, we could all do with a bit of Anil Kumble in ourselves. Play for the team, not for ourselves. Ignore our personal pain, and help the team's cause. Your jaw may be fractured but keep your chin up. Remember that, in the end, we get remembered for our character, attitude and selflessness. The titles, perks, runs and wickets are secondary, and oh-so-fleeting.

And sometimes, our biggest chance for showing our true mettle comes not at the peak of our achievements, but at the nadir of despair. Think about it. Anil had been dropped for the first two Tests. Selected for the third, he broke his jaw before bowling a single ball. Booked to fly back home the next day. Game over. And then he did his heroic fractured-jaw bowling act. He could have stayed in the pavilion. Cursed the captain and selectors for not picking him for the two earlier games. Done last-minute shopping before his premature departure. But all he could really think of was giving 100 per cent. 'At least I tried my best!'

A former Indian CEO has several achievements to his credit: Building the sales system for one of India's largest fast-moving consumer goods companies. Driving its government relationship agenda at a time when government policy significantly hindered MNCs and their businesses in India. And building and leading one of the most passionate sales organizations in an extremely competitive environment. And yet, he is often best remembered for his role in a crisis several years ago. When an entire team of tea plantation executives and their families were held hostage by ultras in Assam, he personally took charge, and against all odds, engineered to airlift the entire group of employees and their families to safety—overnight. Now that's leadership.

Good to remember these leadership lessons. When the chips are down, true leaders don't hide. They stand up and fight. Thanks Anil, for some fine bowling. For some great leadership. And for showing tremendous character. You've meant more to a nation than we'll ever acknowledge.

As a wise man once said, 'For when that great Scorer puts down your name, he doesn't see whether you won or lost—but how you played the game!'

When the chips are down, true leaders don't hide. They stand up and fight. Keep your chin up even if your jaw is broken.

Get into the One-degree-more Habit

Everybody knows that at 99 °C, water is hot. Very hot.

And we also know that at 100 °C, water begins to boil. And becomes steam. And steam is powerful enough to move a trainload of people. Think about it. Just one degree more—and hot water becomes powerful enough to move a locomotive.

While we may not always realize it, our lives are like that too. One degree means a lot. That little extra effort can mean the difference between being a winner and an also-ran. The difference between achieving your goals and missing them. The difference between being just hot water and being able to move a train.

Too often, we give up when the goal might have been just one step away. We finish second, when just one degree more of effort could have meant a world of difference. Unfortunately, we don't have the benefit of a thermometer that can tell us to keep going—for just one degree more. Whatever it is you set out to do, whatever goal you seek to achieve, push yourself to do just a little bit more. Just one degree more. And more often than not, that 'one-degree-more' attitude will mean huge successes in your life.

And just like the difference between being hot water and moving a train, the rewards in life too are disproportionate. Often a fraction of a second can mean the difference between an unforgettable Olympic gold winner and an also-ran. You can lose a five-setter Wimbledon final by a whisker—and find that you earn only half the prize money and none of the honour associated with being a Grand Slam champion. Life is tough. One degree makes a world of a difference.

The next time you feel you've done your bit, or you feel like giving up, stretch yourself. For just one degree more. The difference can be magical. Successful people do all that is expected of them. And then, they do a little bit more.

Make that extra effort. And watch the magic begin!

Get into the 'one-degree-more' habit. The habit of winners. Do all that is expected. And then a little bit more.

IV

WINNER'S MINDSETS

The Power of Positive Expectations

Have you heard of how a group of people decided to set up a Pessimists' Society in London? It was a trendsetting idea, and all the pessimists in the neighbourhood agreed to meet the following Sunday to set up the association. But when the appointed day came, nobody turned up for the meeting. Apparently, they all felt that it just wouldn't work. Ahem!

As negative feelings go, it's widely accepted that pessimism pretty much tops the charts. What is not quite as well accepted is the power of optimism. The power of positive expectations.

While you may have your reservations about *The Secret* type of 'If you think you will get a parking slot near the supermarket, you surely will' assurances, there is evidence to suggest that positive expectations have a powerful impact on outcomes. Have positive expectations—and get positive results! As the following story shows, there may be a powerful lesson in this for all of us.

In an experiment in a school in Texas, USA, the principal came up with a brilliant plan to ensure outstanding results for his school. The top thirty students in Grade 7 were handpicked and put into a class under the supervision of the top three teachers in the school. The objective: to train the students to top the state examination and bring glory to the school.

The teachers got to work in right earnest. Delighted to be selected as the top three in the school, they worked extra hard on their brilliant students. Projects upon projects were assigned, extra classes were held over weekends and the teachers were delighted to help the students individually, to help them ace the state-level examination.

The kids too were enthused. They would quite happily agree to skip the odd baseball game in favour of maths class. Their parents were thrilled to see their wards being selected. Family holidays were postponed to ensure that the kids didn't miss a day of school. The parents took extra care to follow up on homework and assignments. At the end of the year, when the results were declared, it was found that the batch of thirty students had in fact done outstandingly well, ranking in the top percentile of the state's schoolchildren.

A visibly delighted school principal called the three teachers and congratulated them on their achievement.

The teachers were rather self-effacing, preferring to attribute their success to the fabulously talented kids and their diligence. 'It was such a pleasure teaching such exceptionally bright kids!' they concurred.

Then the principal revealed the secret. These kids were NOT exceptional. Not the brightest of the lot. Not by a mile. They were just thirty kids picked at random from across the three divisions and handed over to the three teachers.

The teachers were taken aback but were quick to rationalize—after all, THEY were the three best teachers. They had obviously worked their magic. 'Well, not quite,' revealed the principal. 'I just put all the teachers' names into a hat and pulled out three. And you happened to be those three!'

So what really happened? With thirty average students and three randomly picked teachers, how was the school able to deliver outstanding results? The answer: the power of positive expectations!

The teachers, sensing their special status and the expectations from them, worked extra hard. Longer hours. Better preparation. More projects. They saw sparks of genius in their students, and worked harder to help them shine brighter. And the students, delighted to be hand-picked, slogged harder, made sacrifices and willed themselves to rise to their potential. And the environment—their parents, the school—helped them along.

There's a message here for all of us. As parents. As team leaders. As humans.

Expect more. Expect good things to happen from your team, your spouse, your kids, your world. And you will find them willing themselves to deliver on those positive expectations. Also, don't keep those expectations secret. Share them. Talk about your positive expectations. Let the world know. Don't let the fear of failure—the fear of *what if*—stop you in your tracks.

Expectations have the power of making reality fit in. Tell your child he is clumsy, careless, always dropping stuff . . . And guess what? He will live up to your expectations. Every time he drops something, he will tell himself 'that's me' or 'can't help it, I'm like that'! And later, he'll probably rationalize that 'My parents always told me I was clumsy. They were real quick to spot that in me!'

On the other hand, you can tell him he's really smart, and destined to do well. And then watch him work extra hard to solve those tricky algebra sums. 'I can do it. My dad always tells me I am smart. Maybe I just need to practise harder.' And the harder he practises, well, the smarter he gets.

At work too, the power of positive expectations holds good. Expect your team to do well, and watch them go the extra mile to ensure they don't let you down. So the choice is yours really. Expect good things. And watch it come true. Else, of course, feel free to expect failure. Like many people do.

And like them, you can always say 'I told you so.'

Expect more, get more. Expect failure. And get that too.

Who Stole My Cookies?

It happened one day at Chicago's O'Hare airport.

A young lady was waiting in the departure lounge for the boarding announcement of her delayed flight. It was a Friday evening, and she was looking forward to getting home, and to the dinner date with her boyfriend. Just a wee bit impatient with the delay, she walked across to a kiosk and bought herself a pack of her favourite cookies—almond and raisin specials!

Spotting a seat adjacent to a convenient table-like space, she quickly settled in and pulled out her laptop, hoping to finish the presentation she had been working on. She took one bite of the cookie, then another . . . the cookie was quickly gone! As she reached out for a second cookie, she was taken aback to find that the man on the next seat was helping himself to one too, without even the courtesy of 'May I please . . .'!

What a weird man, she thought to herself, biting into

another cookie. She tried to focus on her work but was quickly distracted by the sight of that shirt sleeve reaching out yet again and grabbing another cookie!

Was he being friendly? Was he being a bully? Was he a thief? A million angry thoughts crossed her mind, and she was tempted to pull the pack of cookies away and give a piece of her mind to the man. She held herself back but only just. She threw him one of those glazed looks that seemed to combine scorn, anger and disgust. The man only smiled.

And this went on. She'd take a cookie, and so would he. Until it was down to the last cookie. As she eyed it, the man quickly grabbed it, split it into two and gave her a half. She took the cookie and was about to stand up, yell and create a scene when she heard the announcement of her flight being ready for departure. She got up, grabbed her bags and headed off towards the boarding gate, still angry, very angry with the man who stole her cookies.

She got into the aircraft, found her way to her window seat and to get her mind off the wretched guy, she decided to immerse herself in a book. 'Better to lose myself in a world of make-believe rather than think of real-world demons!' And she reached into her handbag to pull out her reading glasses . . .

Guess what she found in her handbag? Her pack of cookies. The almond-and-raisin specials! 'Oh no!' she sighed.

Those two words escaped her lips as she sank into her seat. And as she realized what had really transpired, she felt terrible. She had been eating the other guy's cookies! And she'd been so rude to him. And she'd thought he was such a terrible guy. And the man—no, that gentleman, she corrected herself—had smiled through it all, even as a stranger ate his cookies.

She got up instinctively to see if the man was on the same flight, so she could at least apologise for her behaviour and thank him for the cookies. But he was nowhere in sight.

You may think this is a nice little story about a remarkable coincidence involving other people in a faraway land. No! What happened that evening in Chicago between a man, a woman and a pack of cookies happens to you and me, to all of us, all the time. With cookies, or without.

We go through our lives feeling that other people are taking advantage of us, of our talents, stealing our cookies. We seldom pause to think about how we depend on others, on their support, their cookies.

Not just that. Often, the cookies we think of as our own actually belong to others. We worry, we fume when we see someone else get credit for what we think of as 'our achievements'. And yet we happily bask in the glory of recognition for achievements that were clearly the result of other people's support. No problems with that!

Joint ventures and business partnerships are witnesses to several such moments of stolen cookies. Each side feels the other side is stealing its cookies. Success, however, lies in thinking like that man at O'Hare. Share those cookies, and keep smiling.

My friend Devdutt Pattanaik sums it up beautifully. A doctor by training, Devdutt has chosen to pursue his passion for Indian mythology. He draws parallels between mythology and the modern workplace, culling lessons for all of us. He says that the world is full of cows and dogs. More dogs, fewer cows. Cows are the givers. They give their milk, not only to their own calves but also to strangers, to humans. They share happily with everyone, not just their own. Dogs are the takers. Wherever they are, they claim territorial rights. Go near them and they growl, they threaten, they fight for the bone, they fight to claim space that doesn't belong to them. They want those cookies, others' cookies.

Devdutt says every organization, nay the world, needs more cows than dogs. Ask yourself: What are you?

Back to the cookies . . . The next time you feel someone else is eating your cookies, just smile. There will be times when you are like that man, and you'll find someone else eating your cookies. Never mind. Be a cow. Give. Smile.

There will also be times when you'll be like that young lady, eating someone else's cookies, mistaking them for your own. Don't growl. Don't be rude. Just smile.

Clearly, it's a good idea to go through life with a smile. Remember, there will always be another pack of cookies waiting for you somewhere.

We all go through our lives feeling that other people are taking advantage of us, of our talents, stealing our cookies. We seldom pause to think about how we depend on others, their support, their cookies. Often, the cookies we think of as our own actually belong to someone else.

Changing Mindsets. And the Size-15 Shirt!

Driving change is one of the biggest challenges a new leader faces. Often, the arrival of a new leader in an organization is accompanied by a flurry of change. Some of it is anticipated but almost all of it is opposed.

As any new leader will tell you, changing behaviours is tough. And changing mindsets? Phew! Even tougher.

The first challenge is the outsider syndrome. Your advice is disregarded because 'what would you know, we've been doing this for several years. You need to learn, ha ha!' Then there's the familiar tale of 'but it's always been that way!' And then there is the belief that it's worked in the past, so no reason why it won't work in the future.

And, worst of all, in an attempt to resist change, we tend to confuse cause-and-effect linkages. (I love the story of the man who was being lectured on the merits of having a bath every day. 'I wonder how people can have a shower every day!' he remarked. 'I take a shower just once in a month—and yet feel itchy all over!')

We all hold on to our beliefs, steadfastly refusing to let go. And we find dubious linkages to justify our mindsets. We forget those immortal words: 'If you only do what you've always done, you'll only get what you've always got.'

There is that other story of a man who complained of persistent neck pain, severe migraine and frequent dizzy spells. He consulted a doctor, who took a good look at him and pronounced the terrible news: He had only six months to live. The man walked out dejected. But then he decided what the hell, if he had only six months to live, he might as well live it up. And do all those things he always wanted to. First, he decided to get himself six silk shirts. He bought some exquisite silk and went to the finest tailor in town, who began to measure him out. With the measuring tape around the man's collar, the tailor said to his attentive assistant, 'Size 16.'

'No, no,' said the man. 'I'm a size 15.' 'Oh really?' said the tailor. 'Let me check again . . . You are a size 16. No doubt about it.'

'I am a size 15. I have always been a size 15. And I want a size 15!' said the man, rather indignantly. 'So be it,' said the tailor. 'But I must warn you, sir, if you wear size-15 shirts, you will have persistent neck pain, severe migraine and frequent dizzy spells.'

Think about it. We are all like that man. We have our own size-15 hang-ups, our beliefs that we refuse to let go of. Our thinking, which we refuse to change. Ideas, misconceptions that hold us back. And the interesting bit is that in our role as the tailor, we are all quick to spot the problem with other people's collar sizes.

But when it comes to ourselves, we just cannot see the problem with our own shirt sizes! And we suffer for it. The next time you find that things aren't going the way you'd like them to, challenge your thinking. Change your mindset. And change your shirt size.

If you only do what you've always done, you'll only get what you've always got!

Looking through Our Own Glass Windows

Wonder if you've heard the story of the young couple who moved into a new apartment. One morning, the woman looked out of her kitchen window and saw the neighbours' laundry drying on a line. The clothes looked dirty, really dirty. 'I don't think they know how to wash clothes. They look so dirty!' said she to her husband. 'Maybe they use a lousy detergent!' added the husband absent-mindedly, his face still buried in the newspaper.

A few days later, this happened again. Dirty-looking laundry again. Derogatory remarks about the neighbours' incompetence again.

Then, one Sunday morning, the woman was in for a surprise. She looked out of her window and saw really clean laundry. 'Ah!' she exclaimed. 'They finally learnt how to do it right. Perhaps someone taught them how to wash clothes!'

'Actually, dear,' said her husband, 'I got up early this morning and cleaned our windows.'

Ouch! What's true for the couple is true for all of us too. It only confirms what behavioural scientists have maintained all along. We see things not the way they are but the way *we* are! Our windows—our tinted glasses—significantly impact our view of the world.

We all see other people through our own stained-glass windows. If we are looking for faults, we find them. Just as easily as we'd find good if we go looking for that. So it helps not to jump to conclusions and damn other people. It may not be them; our own windows may be to blame.

This is true not just of other people, but of life itself. If you've lived with the fear of failure all your life, you tend to erect a window of risk aversion. In every opportunity, you first see the risks, the downsides, the possibility of failure. Someone else may look at the same image through the window of optimism and see a huge, overpowering silver lining.

A man pulled into a petrol pump on a highway. 'What are the people like in the town ahead?' he asked the attendant. The attendant replied, 'What were they like in the town you are coming from?' 'Awful!' said the man. 'Rude, cold and unfriendly.' 'Well,' said the attendant, 'I'm sorry but you'll find that the people in the town ahead are the same.'

A while later, another car headed in the same direction pulled in. 'What are the people like in the town ahead?' the driver asked the attendant. 'What were they like in the town you are coming from?' repeated the attendant. 'Wonderful,' said the man, 'warm, helpful and friendly!' 'Well,' said the attendant, 'I'm happy to say that you'll find that the people in the town ahead are the same.'

It's always like that. It's not about them, it's about us. It's not the world, it's the window.

For you to start seeing opportunities, the world around you need not change. Just the windows through which you see your world need realignment or a bit of cleaning! Our windows are made out of our experiences, our biases. We are quick to form opinions of others, based on fleeting perceptions, based on the view from our own windows.

The next time you find fault with someone, pause before you proceed to damn them. Perhaps it's time to clean your windows!

We see things not the way they are, but the way *we* are!

So What's Your White Rabbit?

I love this story of the man in a beautiful town house in a place far, far away. I love it because it's the story of your life. And mine. And everyone else's.

Seems the man was an honest hard-working bloke, who never hurt a fly. Pleased with his good work, a fairy magically appeared before him and told him that all the wealth and riches he wanted in life were now within his reach.

'Just go out into the garden,' said the fairy. 'There's a large treasure chest there, filled with gold and diamonds and rubies and other precious gems. Go claim it—it's all yours!' Then she added: 'There's just one catch. There's a white rabbit in the garden. As you go looking for the treasure chest, you must not think about the white rabbit. If you do, you won't be able to find the riches.'

We are all like that man with the white rabbit.

Our goals, our dreams and our just deserts are all

within our reach. But we are held back by our self-limiting beliefs. Our own white rabbits, which prevent us from rising to our full potential and achieving our goals. Which stop us from doing what it takes to get to our goals. 'I can't because . . .' we tell ourselves, and the white rabbit gets going.

We blame it on our childhood, background, education, current situation, boss, spouse, family, employer . . . Whatever. We find our own white rabbits.

And then we get together with others and compare our white rabbits. There's comfort in blaming our white rabbits. And wallowing in self-pity. As we compare our white rabbits and focus on them, they grow stronger.

So what's your white rabbit? Your favourite excuse for not doing what it takes to achieve your goals? Whatever it is, it's good to identify it. And banish it from your mind. Forever.

Remember, there's a treasure chest waiting to be claimed! Banish the self-limiting belief, forget the white rabbit. And claim your fortune!

What's your white rabbit? What prevents you from rising to your full potential and achieving your goals?

V

GIVING

Becoming a Two-dollar Man

One of my life gurus was a man called Jim Rohn. He was the grand old man of American motivational speaking. And a man who significantly helped shape my own philosophy in life. Jim Rohn passed away in December 2009.

I got an interesting piece of advice from him, which I found quite fascinating. It's simple. And yes, it works.

'Become a two-dollar man!' advised Jim.

What exactly did he mean, you might wonder. Let me explain.

According to him the next time that I needed to tip someone, say a dollar, I should give him two dollars instead. Learn to tip two dollars every time, where one dollar might suffice. Do this, not because of what that one extra dollar might mean to the waiter or the bellboy, but for what it will do to you!

When you tip that extra dollar, you begin to 'feel' like

a large-hearted man, like a rich and successful chap. You walk just a bit taller, smile a wider smile and seem like a man in control of his world. And as you walk back into the restaurant the next time, you feel the waiter is giving you that smile of recognition—reinforcing your sense of self-worth. All this, you will agree, is not bad value for just one dollar more!

And often, when you tip just one dollar—the stipulated norm, the bare minimum—you could come away feeling like a bit of a heel. A man who hides the tip in the bill folder, hoping no one will notice. Ah, well, you rationalize, so many people come to this restaurant, surely the waiters wouldn't really know or care about who gave how much. You slink away, hoping nobody notices. But one key person clearly has noticed. You, yourself! And when that happens, there are no hiding places.

So really the habit of tipping that extra dollar is not about what it does to the recipient (sure, it makes him feel good too) but about what it does to you, the giver. About the magic it works on you. And that's worth way more than a dollar.

It's like that with praise too. And love. And recognition. Learn to give more. Just that bit more. Learn to give more credit, more praise, more love. And see how good that makes you feel. The more you give, the richer you'll feel.

It's a good lesson to remember. Giving away an extra

dollar can actually make you richer. Far more than you'd imagine.

Become a two-dollar man. Start today. And see the difference it makes to you!

Learn to give more. Just a bit more. Tipping that extra dollar is not about what it does to the recipient (sure, it makes him feel good) but about what it does to you, the giver.

Bringing Back the Binaca Smile

If you were around in India in the 1960s and 1970s, you'll probably remember a toothpaste brand called Binaca.

In those days, if a little kid or a pretty woman flashed a smile, people would quickly brand it a Binaca smile. Advertisements for Binaca toothpaste famously, and quite memorably, captured the moment with that magical phrase: 'The Binaca Smile'. It never went out of fashion.

There's a lesson to be learnt from Binaca's heady success. A lesson that's relevant even today, long after the toothpaste itself has vanished—from retail shelves, from our lives, even from our memories.

Time then, for a flashback.

Binaca was a rather popular toothpaste brand in those days. It came in a blue and white—or was it blue and yellow?—carton, and held out the promise of strong teeth, healthy gums and a Binaca smile. What's more, every carton had a surprise gift inside! A little plastic animal figurine. A different one in every pack. I still vividly recall the sense of expectation and surprise, as we opened the carton to pull out a new animal. A new surprise, time after time!

It wasn't unusual to visit a friend's place and find a mini-zoo in the showcase, courtesy Binaca. We'd trade duplicates, discuss our newest additions, admire the wonderful new giraffe—and never cease to be enthralled by those teeny-weeny plastic animals.

While the Binaca folks delivered consistent, good quality toothpaste month after month after month, the trick really lay in the surprise gift. That little animal figurine probably cost the toothpaste manufacturer very little, but meant so much to consumers. It held the magic of surprise! Brushing your teeth, with Binaca or anything else, was drudgery. But the joy of opening a Binaca carton to see the animal tucked inside? Incomparable!

In our lives, we do everything in a programmed manner, and tend to miss out on the zing, the surprise element, the little animal in the box. At work, bosses expect consistency, dependability, solid performances. Throw in a little extra, and you will soon be on the fast track. Consistent performance is a given. But ask yourself, what's your little animal figurine?

As customers, we're like that too. We want a dependable brand and consistent quality and yet, we like to be surprised. One of my family's favourite restaurants in

Mumbai, All Stir Fry, serves up consistently nice make-your-own-wok meals. My daughter loves to go back, partly for the wok and perhaps partly for the little fortune cookie they give us at the end. The meal is good. And reading the individual predictions inside the fortune cookie? Even better!

With our loved ones too, we would do well to go beyond the routine and come up with a little surprise here and there. Dads and husbands, moms and wives—they all need to be trusted, to be completely dependable. But hey, add a little surprise, and you add magic to the relationship. Anniversary dinners are great, but they are expected. Predictable. Try taking your wife out for lunch on a busy working day instead—just like that. Or take all your kid's friends out for some sugar candy on the beach. Just like that. Little surprises can be quite magical in their impact.

Delivering toothpaste of consistent quality is good but seldom good enough. Success comes when you combine dependability and awe, predictability and surprise. The surprise can never be a substitute for dependability but it makes for a wonderful value-add. For bosses. For consumers. For loved ones.

We all need to come up with little plastic animals. Remember, these freebies don't cost much but they make a huge difference. Pick up the phone and speak to a friend you haven't spoken to in years. Send little thank you notes to your colleagues. Send a piece of that homemade cake to that neighbour-you-don't-always-meet. If you didn't do any of these—no one would notice. But if you do—they'd never forget! Think of the joy you'd be providing when someone else reminisces on the memories of those surprise moments—putting together all those little figurines you've given them. Imagine watching them show off those little surprises that they have so lovingly collected over the years! Pure magic.

Go for it. Create your own surprise animal-in-the-box. Bring back the Binaca smile.

At work, bosses expect consistency, dependability, solid performances. Throw in a little extra, and you will soon be on the fast track. Consistent performance is a given. But ask yourself, what's your little plastic animal figurine? It doesn't cost much but it makes a huge difference.

The Long (Spoon) and Short of Life

From my days of growing up as a little kid in Jaipur, one of my fondest memories is of the entire family huddled under a blanket on a cold winter evening, listening to tales from Indian mythology that my father would narrate. As the heater whirred in the quiet of the night, the five of us sat under a large blanket on the bed; the need for warmth ensured that we didn't elbow for more space on the bed but in fact jostled to get closer, to get warmer.

The tales were about gods and demons, sacrifices and rewards, heroes and villains. And about good and evil, heaven and hell. Here's one of those heaven-and-hell stories that I often replay in my mind, a bit like a Hindi film flashback . . .

A holy man was speaking to the Lord one day and asked Him the difference between heaven and hell. 'Come, I'll show you,' said the Lord, as he led the man up to two doors.

He pushed open the first door and they entered a large room. A group of people was sitting around a large round table. And on the table was a large pot filled with delicious stew. The aroma made the holy man's mouth water but he noticed that the people looked famished and sickly. They were all holding spoons with long handles, strapped to their arms. While they could all reach out and take spoonfuls of the delicious stew from the pot, they could not put them into their mouths, as the handles were longer than their arms! Their suffering was unbearable, made worse by the wonderful aroma. 'That's hell!' said the Lord.

'Now let's look at heaven,' he said, leading the man through the second door into another identical room. Same round table. Same pot of stew. Same aroma that made the holy man's mouth water. Here too, the people at the table had long spoons strapped to their arms. But they all looked healthy and happy, and were laughing and enjoying themselves.

'I don't get it,' said the holy man. 'Similar rooms, tables, pots, the same stew and identical long spoons. How come these guys are plump and happy, while those people were starved and sad?'

'Simple,' said the Lord. 'These people have learnt to feed each other. The greedy think only of themselves.'

End of flashback.

Wow! Someone has rightly said that you can achieve

all your goals—if only you help enough people achieve their goals. Winning teams and winners are really all about people feeding each other. About putting other people's needs and interests before your own.

The good news is that we all have it in our power to create our own hell or heaven. The rooms, pots, stews, spoons are all the same, for all of us. Trying to feed yourself or learning to feed each other—that's our choice.

So hey, do something really selfish today. Help other people!

You can achieve all your goals, if only you help enough other people achieve theirs.

Gandhi and the One-shoe Syndrome

One of the most celebrated stories from the life of Mahatma Gandhi is about his train journey in South Africa. The story of his first brush with Apartheid, and how he was thrown off a train meant only for whites.

And one of my favourite stories from the life of the Mahatma is also set on a train. This one's not so well known though. But, for me, it defines what made him a true giant among men.

It concerns a rail journey that the young Gandhi was to undertake on his return to India. He waited at the railway platform for the train to arrive. In those days, it was not unusual for the British rail company to stop the train at a station only if some whites wanted to get on, or off. In case there were no white passengers, the train would simply slow down at the station, and Indians—old and young—would scramble on to (or off) the still moving train.

And it so happened that as the young Gandhi climbed on to the moving train, one of his shoes slipped off. As he bent to try and grab it, it slithered down to the track, while the train gathered momentum. In a flash, Gandhi reached for his other shoe and threw it towards the fast disappearing other shoe on the track.

A perplexed onlooker wondered aloud if Gandhi had indeed lost it completely. Gandhi explained: 'Ah well, if someone is to find one of my shoes, hopefully he'll find the other one too, and thus have a fine new pair for himself!'

What a man. What a wonderful instinctive response!

In this age of scams and greed and never-ending wants and the growing multitude of the unhappy rich, it strikes me that we can all take a leaf out of the Mahatma's book.

If you or I were in the Mahatma's shoes (literally!), how would we have reacted? Probably felt miserable for the rest of the journey, at the loss of a new shoe. Complained about the callousness of the railway system. Cursed the engine driver who had caused the loss. Worried about how we'd manage once we reached our destination. That one lost shoe would have played on our mind all the way, piling on the misery.

Unfortunately, we tend to focus on what we don't have. Our mind zeroes in on what we've lost. That other shoe. And we carry that burden of loss, adding to our woes. When instead we could so easily focus on what we have—and see if that could be of use to someone. Giving away that second shoe didn't just make some poor Indian happy (remember, a shoe was quite a luxury for most of our countrymen in those days), it made Gandhi happy too.

Perhaps it's time we all shifted focus. Instead of jostling to become go-getters—wanting more, more, more—we ought to learn to become go-givers. Learning to give. Learning to share. Instead of spending our waking lives worrying about the shoe that got away, perhaps we should thank God for the shoe we still have, and discover how giving it away could make us, and someone else, happier.

It's not just about material possessions. It's like that with love too. And respect. Learning to give, rather than longing for more, could make all of us happier. And the world a better place.

This 'go-giving' attitude has to become second nature. Instinctive almost. It would not have helped Gandhiji to have realized half an hour into the train ride that the solitary shoe was of no use—and he might as well give it away. It worked because he thought of it right there, right then.

Too often, we find ourselves discussing in the comfort of our homes how we should have—could have—helped someone. Done our bit. When the moment passes, the opportunity sadly vanishes too.

So here's an action commitment to make, today. Become a go-giver. Not a go-getter. Help someone. Share what you have. And discover the joys of not having to worry about the shoe that got away.

Become a go-giver, not a go-getter.

VI

HARD WORK

Navjot Sidhu: From Strokeless Wonder to Palm Tree Hitter!

An air of expectation blows in every organization when annual appraisal season comes around. Appraisal time is time for performance feedback, and time for increments and bonuses.

Traditionally, organizations have combined the feedback exercise with the annual salary revision ritual. I suspect this has reduced the efficacy of performance feedback as a powerful developmental tool.

It doesn't help that, culturally, Indians have tended to be rather poor at delivering (and receiving) critical feedback. We are taught to be nice guys; when a gracious hostess asks how the coffee is, we say it's nice even if we feel it tastes like lukewarm cough syrup mixed with leftover soup! In our effort to make sure that the feedback is well received, we sugar-coat it. So much so that all that the recipient gets is sugar-coating, and the bitter pill is missed out.

Truth is, criticism and critics could play a huge, huge role in improving our performance. In helping you rise to your full potential. I remember my college-going daughter returning from work at a radio station where she was an intern. Her immediate supervisor was being rather harsh on her. She was reduced to tears, wondering why he was picking on her and continuously criticizing her performance. She spoke to the human resources head, who told her this: 'It's a good thing he's doing that. When you make mistakes and no one tells you anything, it means they are giving up on you. You may not like to hear it but he's actually telling you that he cares. He believes you can do better. He wants you to do better, to be the best you can.'

There's another powerful role a critic can play at times. He can challenge you to prove him wrong, inspire you to raise your performance and do what you may have been capable of but never accomplished.

Navjot Singh Sidhu, former Indian cricketer perhaps better known for his witticisms on TV than his exploits on the field, tells an inspiring story. Sidhu made his debut in Test cricket against the West Indies in 1983. In three innings, he managed a high score of 20, in a painstakingly long stay of 114 minutes. The critics were trenchant and well-known cricket writer Rajan Bala (alas, now no more) famously branded Navjot the 'strokeless wonder' in an article in *Indian Express*. Not surprisingly, Sidhu was dropped soon after from the Indian squad. And confined to the unfancied backwaters of first-class cricket in India.

Navjot was born into an affluent family, and he tells a story from his early years. His father would wake him at 5 a.m. and ask him to go for a jog. Navjot would get up and once his father was out of sight, he'd bribe his servants to let him sleep in another room. At 7 a.m., he'd wake up, splash water on his face and shirt and present himself looking all sweaty before his father. Impressed by his hard work, Sidhu Senior would encourage his *sher da puttar* to take some well-earned rest. And Navjot would go right back to bed!

When Sidhu was dropped from the team in 1983, after just two Tests, his father brought him the newspaper with Rajan Bala's article and left it on his bed, without uttering a word. Young Navjot was devastated. He cut out the article and pasted it on his closet. The 'strokeless wonder' tag would stare down at him, every waking moment.

That one article, the accusation of being a 'strokeless wonder', the criticism from a senior cricket writer, seemed to set off something inside Sidhu. And he was determined to prove his critics wrong. He was determined to take fresh guard and shed the tag of being a shirker. Forever. He took it upon himself to turn things around. He resolved to become a cricketer his father and his country would be proud of.

Now when his father came into Navjot's room to wake him up at 5 a.m., he was already gone. He was out in the nets at 5 a.m., having already jogged a bit. He practised hitting sixes and smashing the ball around, keen to become an attacking stroke player, not a strokeless wonder. His target: hit 300 sixes, every day. He still paid bribes though—not to his servants to let him sleep a few extra winks but to young lads, as an incentive to bowl at him late into the night, to allow him to complete his daily quota of 300 sixes. At the end of the day, his gloves were soaking wet, with sweat and even blood at times.

Four years is a long time to be out of the India team. Most players would have given up on their dream of playing again for India. Not Navjot Singh Sidhu. After four years in the wilderness, Sidhu was recalled to play for India. He was, in fact, selected to play for India in the 1987 World Cup. And what a comeback it was! In his first game, against the formidable Aussies, Sidhu scored 73 runs off 79 balls, with 5 sixes and 4 fours! He went on to score 50s in his first four One-day innings, with a strike rate of over 90.

The newspaper clipping stayed on the closet but the 'strokeless wonder' tag was history. Wiped out by determination. By blood, sweat and toil. Sidhu went on to play with distinction for India: over 4400 runs in 137 One-day games with an average of 37.08. And yes, 44 sixes! And in his Test match career, Sidhu played 51 tests, hit 9 centuries, aggregated over 3200 runs and averaged a respectable 42.13. And the crowning glory? A certain Mr Rajan Bala wrote about how a 'strokeless wonder' had become a 'palm tree hitter'.

The next time someone criticizes you, remember you have two options. You can either sulk and give up, complaining about how unfair the world is and how your efforts go unnoticed. Or you could get back to work on your shortcomings and flaws, and emerge a winner. The choice is yours.

Rajan Bala may not have realized it but his criticism actually helped Sidhu shake off the cobwebs of complacency and become a successful cricketer. It sparked off a new determination, a new resolve. It led to long hours of practice. To 300 sixes a day. And all that blood, sweat and toil created one of India's most attacking stroke-makers.

It worked for Sidhu. And it can work for you too.

You may not want to hear it, but your critics are often the ones telling you that they love you and care about you, and want to make you better.

Lessons in Survival from Frogs and Phelps

A crisis is a true test of character, they say. And given how several people find themselves in a crisis these days, it's useful to remember some basic lessons in surviving, nay thriving in, troubled times. Ups and downs are a part of business and of life but how you tackle the downs holds the key to the highs that might occur later in life.

A business you started could run into trouble. Or you could find yourself laid off. It happens. You may find yourself burdened with some emotional upheaval. Or a health problem that lays you low. In such cases, it is important to ensure that you don't get petrified into inaction like a deer caught in a car's headlights. You must keep moving, keep fighting, keep trying. Sure, merely fighting hard in what looks like a hopeless situation won't guarantee success. But remember, not trying—and simply giving up—will only guarantee failure. When you find yourself with your back to the wall, when you feel you are going deeper and farther into a deep black hole, it's a good idea to remind yourself of that fidgety frog and the pail of milk.

Seems there was this frog, ever curious about the world around him. As he hopped about in the farmer's house, discovering a new world, he accidentally landed in a pail of fresh milk. He tried to jump out but the walls were way too high. He tried to push himself off the bottom of the pail but it was far too deep. With milk clouding his vision, and really no hope of survival, you would excuse the frog for thinking his end was near. Elders would have admonished him for his carelessness, some even suggesting that he deserved his plight.

But the frog was not about to give up. He kicked, he squirmed, he splashed. Like his life depended on it. As it indeed did. His legs began to ache but the frog kept kicking, splashing, squirming, even though there was no hope in sight. All that churning eventually had its impact, as the milk turned into a lump of butter. The frog jumped on top of the butter—and escaped to freedom!

When you are down in the dumps, remember to keep kicking, to keep fighting. What you do in these difficult times will determine what happens to you next.

Not only could this be the key to your survival, it could potentially be a life changer. If you find you're suddenly fired, don't fret. It may just be the perfect opportunity to hone a new skill or develop a latent talent that can make a huge difference to your life. People have switched careers and turned to teaching, writing, farming—and discovered far more joy in their new-found vocations than their earlier jobs with fat pay cheques and fancy titles could have ever given them. In their most difficult hour, people have started businesses that brought them unimagined wealth. Perhaps it's your turn now to take the plunge. That moment of strife, that hour of darkness, those crisis-ridden days could be the opportunity to craft a new beginning, a new triumph.

Some months before Michael Phelps swam his way to Olympic immortality with eight gold medals in Beijing, he was involved in an unfortunate accident that seriously jeopardized his Olympic dreams. In October 2007, as Michael was getting into a friend's car in Michigan, he slipped on a patch of ice and fell, breaking his wrist. Interesting sidelight: Michael may be fabulously graceful in water but on ground, he is apparently an extremely awkward mover, perennially prone to slipping. Life is like that. Great swimmer, lousy walker. You win some, you lose some. But rather than worry about his inability to walk with grace and stability, he focuses on doing what comes naturally—swimming. And that makes all the difference!

Back to the accident. A cracked wrist meant a plaster

cast—a serious blow to his Olympics preparation. He couldn't swim for the next few weeks. He was shattered. Was the great eight-gold Olympic dream over? All those years of practice, would they come to naught? After his fabulous showing in Athens, Michael had the world's eyes trained on him—and he was a hot favourite for bagging an unparalleled eight-gold haul. Was the accident the start of the end?

Michael was disillusioned but quickly picked himself up and was back in the pool. With his plastered arm, he couldn't swim but he would lie in the pool, kicking with a kickboard while his Olympic teammates did laps. He just splashed and kicked away furiously. While that was no substitute for swimming, it had one huge positive. He added incredible strength to his leg muscles.

Fast forward to 16 August 2008, in Beijing. Having won six golds, Michael Phelps was on track to the eight-gold dream. Just two races to go. In the seventh event, the 100 metre butterfly stroke event, Michael was neck and neck with Milorad Cavic. He won by the narrowest of margins, picking up his seventh gold by edging out Milorad by a mere hundredth of a second. That's right—the margin was a hundredth of a second! As experts analysed the race and watched slow-motion replays, they found that in the last 5 metres of the race, while an exhausted Milorad dragged his legs, Michael used a strong kick to get his hands to the wall first, going ahead by that hundredth of a second. That strong final kick made the difference. Those leg-strengthening exercises paid off!

It doesn't matter whether you are a frog or the world's greatest swimmer ever. The lesson is the same. When you are down and in trouble, keep fighting. Don't give up. Keep kicking. It won't help to wallow in self-pity, or curse your stars or play the blame game. Every adversity has an opportunity couched within. It is up to us to grab it. And what you do when the going gets tough, is what defines your outcomes.

You could give up trying to scale the walls of the pail—and drown in the milk. You could give up on your Olympic ambitions and blame it on an untimely injury. Or you could choose to keep kicking away and turn the milk into butter, and make it a lifesaver. You could keep kicking away and strengthen your leg muscles, which could one day help make you the world's greatest swimmer.

Perhaps this explains, in a somewhat convoluted way, the origin of the phrase 'alive and kicking'! Get a life. Keep kicking!

When you are down and in trouble, keep fighting. Don't give up. Keep kicking. What you do in these difficult times often determines what happens next.

Learning to Fly: Lessons from a Butterfly

The incredible transformation of creepy-crawly caterpillars into amazingly colourful butterflies is one of the marvels of nature. As the caterpillar forms a cocoon—and then emerges from it as a butterfly—it holds out a valuable reminder for all of us. Don't be dismissive of seemingly ordinary, average performers. There might just be a butterfly in them, waiting to emerge!

There's an even more powerful life lesson hidden in this natural phenomenon, as the following story shows.

A man was sitting in a garden when he saw the incredible sight of a cocoon with a tiny opening through which a butterfly was trying to emerge. He watched for over an hour, captivated, as the butterfly struggled to come out of that tiny hole, bit by bit, flapping its wings, shaking itself, fighting, struggling to free its body. But even after an hour of frantic struggling, it seemed that the poor little insect was making no progress. It had probably got as far as it could on its own.

So the man decided to help the poor butterfly. With gentle hands, he tore open the hole in the cocoon, just a bit wider to allow the butterfly to emerge easily. The butterfly came out. It had a shrivelled body and tiny wings. It looked weak and tender.

The man eagerly waited for the butterfly's wings to open up and expand, for it to fly away. But that did not happen. In fact, the butterfly stayed weak and shrivelled, unable to fly.

The man did not realize that in his attempt to help the butterfly, he had in fact harmed it. The struggle to break free from the cocoon is nature's way of preparing the butterfly to learn to fly. As it fights to emerge from the restrictive cocoon, fluids from the body get pushed into the wings, making them stronger, making them larger, enabling them to fly. Without that struggle, the butterfly stays weak and unable to fly.

No struggle, no success. That's as true for butterflies as it is for all of us.

Struggles and challenges make us stronger, more capable. The next time you find yourself struggling and feel like giving up, remember it may be nature's way of helping you fly and soar to your true potential. At times, you may find that a dear friend or your boss or your mentor is deserting you in your hour of need. Don't be too harsh on them. They may be doing it to help you, to help your wings develop fully, so that you learn to fly.

One of my fondest memories of my career revolves around my first few months as a management trainee at Hindustan Lever. As part of the training programme, you start off as a frontline salesman, selling soap and toothpaste and shampoo. The sales stint requires all trainees—freshly minted from blue-chip B-schools—to spend the first few months living the salesman's life. You live in lodges in small towns on salesman's allowances. You travel by bus and train and get a first-hand feel of the real thing. Another incredible learning experience in those days was my two-month rural stint, living in Etah district of Uttar Pradesh, getting a taste of how 70 per cent of the country lives. Those experiences, I believe, helped us all emerge stronger, become better human beings and smarter managers. Corporate India has seen some of its finest leaders emerge from the 'Hindustan Lever School of Management'. Those early days of struggle, no doubt, played their part in the process.

In cricket, Suresh Raina is perhaps the latest example of the cocoon syndrome.

Seen as a precocious talent, Raina found himself pitch-forked into the Indian squad, without going through the real grind of first-class cricket. After a brief stint on the team, where he promised much but delivered little, he was dropped. Then, he went out and pushed himself through the hard yards of first-class domestic cricket. For eighteen rigorous months. After consistent performances there, he fought his way back into the team—and has only improved ever since!

Not all of us are as lucky as Raina though. We don't always get a second chance to return to first base. The tiny, shrivelled butterfly can't choose to go back into the cocoon and fight its way out to strengthen its wings.

The next time you find yourself struggling, remember it might just be your preparation for take-off. When you get that chance to struggle, make the most of it. After all, in dictionaries and in life, success never comes before struggle.

The next time you find yourself struggling and feel like giving up, remember it may be nature's way of helping you fly and soar to your true potential. No struggle, no success.

VII

THE WINNER'S WAY

Goalkeepers and the Action Bias

My son is a football fan. Okay, not just a fan. He's crazy about the game. As we watch the English Premier League games on TV in his room, which is increasingly looking like a museum of Manchester United merchandise, my fascination for the sport grows. A new fan is emerging, slowly but surely.

One aspect of the game that has caught my fancy is the penalty kick. I love to put myself in the footballer's shoes, and try to simulate the pressure he must be experiencing. I often think that the penalty kick mirrors life itself, in many ways. Think of the poor goalkeeper. Someone else commits a foul, and the goalkeeper is left trying to block a goal, paying for another's folly! And the striker who is taking the penalty kick? Poor soul. He knows he is expected to score. If he does, no big deal. If he doesn't, God help him!

I have also discovered that I'm not alone in my

fascination with penalty kicks. I came across a piece of research by a team of scholars in Israel. To understand the goalkeeper's mindset, the team studied 286 penalty kicks from major league football games around the world. As you probably know, a penalty kick is taken from a distance of just 11 metres from the goal. The goalkeeper gets about 0.1 second to react—a window so tiny that goalkeepers must guess which way the ball will go, and commit themselves to a dive—left or right.

The research team tracked the direction of the kick (left, right or centre) and tabulated the statistics. And here's what it found: A goalkeeper's best chance of blocking a penalty kick is if he doesn't dive but just stays put in the centre! You wouldn't have guessed that, would you?

That's not all. Though the probability of stopping a kick is highest when the goalkeeper did not move, the team found that in 92 per cent of the cases, the goalkeeper committed himself to a dive on either side. Why was that? Goalkeepers in professional football are highly paid, highly accomplished, highly intelligent. Why then do they dive, when standing still would give them their best chance of success?

The answer apparently lies in the bias for action that most sportspeople—and high achievers—have. If the goalkeeper stands still and lets slip a goal, he is subject to ridicule. 'He didn't even try!' comes the anguished cry from friends and fans. But if he dives, the view is more sympathetic: 'He tried. There's not much you can do when someone is firing a shot from 11 metres!'

So match after match, when a penalty kick is taken, goalkeepers around the world dive. And inevitably fail to stop a goal from being scored. When standing still could perhaps spell success!

What's true for goalkeepers is true for many of us too. We get conditioned by our bias for action. We get restless, we feel compelled to act. Standing still is seen as a sign of weakness. Inaction is generally not looked upon favourably. We fall prey to the action bias and feel compelled to choose between two alternative paths. In reality, it might have helped had we created option three: Stand still!

And this happens all the time. Take advertising for instance. Some of the most memorable advertising campaigns have been stopped prematurely to be replaced by newer campaigns that just don't have the same magic. Why? Perhaps because some young brand manager fears that if he continues with the campaign and sales plummet and shares drop, he'll be hanged for not doing anything. However, if he ran a new campaign and sales dropped . . . Well, at least he did something, didn't he?

This irresistible urge explains why fund managers churn the portfolio so regularly. It also explains CEO behaviour. Notice how CEOs are always busy—acquiring a new business, divesting something, upsizing or downsizing, decentralizing operations, pulling the strings back into the head office launching new brands, or killing old ones. Chances are, the businesses would be better off if the CEOs actually choose the elusive option: Doing nothing.

It's good for all of us to remember the lesson from the research on penalty kicks, and stop thinking like goalkeepers usually do. While a bias for action is good to have (good goalies are forever diving and making spectacular saves), in several situations it pays to just stand still.

Doing nothing can sometimes be the best thing you can do!

At times, standing still is the best action you can take!

Of Sharks, Pepsi and the Comfort Zone

If there were a travel advisory aimed specifically at leaders, there's one place they would be strongly advised against entering: the Comfort Zone.

Getting complacent, feeling invincible and floating in the comfort zone of 'been there, done that' can deflate not just an individual but an entire organization, resulting in a rapid decline in individual and team performance. Cruise control may be a fabulous feature in cars and aeroplanes but it can be quite a spoiler in human beings.

Successful people constantly prod themselves out of the comfort zone—by posing new challenges, by constantly raising the bar, by changing contexts. Steve Waugh, former Australian cricket captain, who so successfully pushed himself and his team to consistently perform at the peak, called his autobiography *Out of the Comfort Zone*. Competition, the threat of defeat, the prospect of winning and the looming figure of a competitor can all ensure that you avoid getting stuck in the comfort zone.

In the corporate world, the cola wars probably best exemplified this phenomenon. In India, for instance, both Coke and Pepsi built up passionate teams—armies, in fact—where the vision was as much about finishing off the enemy as it was about gaining market share. Given the nature of the business, there was no time to rest on laurels. Victory and defeat were decided every moment in nondescript stores in far-flung towns across the country—every time a consumer walked up and asked for a cola. You were only as good as the last bottle sold. The presence of a strong competitor meant that the entire sales organization had a unique passion, a fire-in-the-belly approach imprinted in its corporate DNA. There used to be a line attributed to a planner in Coke's headquarters that probably summed it up: 'If there were no Pepsi, we would have had to invent it!'

R. Gopalakrishnan, former vice chairman of Hindustan Unilever and currently executive director of Tata Sons, narrates an interesting story in his book, *The Case of the Bonsai Manager*. It's about fish in Japan. And the message is relevant for individuals and corporates around the world.

It's a classic problem–solution saga that the Japanese love to relate. As is well known, the Japanese love fresh fish. Such has been Japan's fascination with eating fresh fish that, for many years now, there's hardly any fish to be found in the waters off Japanese shores. So fishermen came up with a solution. They built bigger boats and went farther from the shore to catch fish. Unfortunately, this created another problem. The farther they went to fish, the longer it took them to get back to the shore. By the time they got back, the fish was stale. And the Japanese, well, they like their fish fresh.

To solve this problem, the fishermen came up with another solution. They installed refrigeration units on the boats. But the Japanese were clearly clever, discerning folks. They could tell the difference between frozen fish and fresh fish. And they wanted their fresh fish. Besides, frozen fish commanded lower prices, threatening the viability of the entire fishing business.

So the fishermen came up with another solution. They installed fish tanks on the boat! They would catch fish from the sea and put them into the tank. So they could now take back fresh fish!

But that was not to be either. As the tank got stuffed with fish, the fish would flap around a bit, then get lazy and lie resigned to their fate. Motionless. Inactive. Dull. And the Japanese could tell the difference. They wanted fresh fish, not sluggish fish!

Even as a seemingly insurmountable crisis loomed over the Japanese fishing industry, the wise fisherfolk came up with yet another innovative solution. They still had to sail out a long distance. And they still had the same boats and the same fish tanks. But there was one difference. In each tank, the fishermen put in a small shark. The shark kept the fish active, running around, busy. Sure, the shark ate a few fish but the threat of the shark kept the other fish active and healthy. The challenge ensured that none of them could afford to lie still. As a result, what eventually reached the shore was fresh, active fish. And the Japanese loved it!

We are like fish too. We need that shark to stay sharp. In case you or your organization is slowly slipping into the comfort zone, it may be a good idea to bring in a shark. If you are Coke, invent a Pepsi. Do what Steve Waugh did constantly to himself and his team—get outta the comfort zone! Remember, the shark may eat some fish but that's a small price to pay for keeping the rest of them active. Get your shark. Today!

Get out of the comfort zone. If there's no enemy, create one.

Taking for Granted: Lessons from F Words!

Take this simple test. Read the sentence below, and see how many Fs you can find:

FINISHED FILES ARE THE RE-
SULT OF YEARS OF SCIENTI-
FIC STUDY COMBINED WITH
THE EXPERIENCE OF YEARS.

So how many did you count? Three? Four? Or five? If you counted six, congratulations. You are a genius. In fact, you've done as well as an average seven-year-old.

Truth is that when this test is administered to grown-ups, less than 5 per cent get it right. (And some among them have probably seen this before!) There are indeed six Fs. And here they are, highlighted for you!

FINISHED **F**ILES ARE THE RE-
SULT O**F** YEARS O**F** SCIENTI**F**-
IC STUDY COMBINED WITH
THE EXPERIENCE O**F** YEARS.

So why do adults get it wrong, while kids can get it right in a jiffy? Experts reckon it's got to do with the way the adult mind gets conditioned to reading the F sound. Our minds tend to miss the F in 'of'. It's there but several years of reading fast—and latching on to F sounds in words like 'finish' and 'files', and missing it in words like 'of'—result in adults not counting the Fs accurately. In trying to read faster, we notice a few Fs and miss out on the others, which our minds take for granted.

If you think about it carefully, it's not just F words that we take for granted. There are several things in our lives that our conditioned minds miss out on. As we spend all our waking hours chasing Fame and Fortune (Ah, F words again!), there are some other Fs that we take for granted, ignore, lose sight of . . .

Like Friends. Family. Faith. And Fun!

They are there, all the time. But in our scramble for Fast cars and Fast cash and Fame and Fortune, the mind loses sight of them. Important as they may be, the mind takes them for granted. And ignores them.

Perhaps it's time to bring back the innocence of a seven-year-old. Time to rediscover our real strengths. And as you notch up the points for Fame and Fortune in your personal balance sheet, it may be a good idea to check the real score. And look hard for those other Fs—Family, Friends, Faith, Fun—that are there but probably being taken for granted.

Years of neglect and of being taken for granted may make these Fs hard to spot but they are there. Waiting to be seen. And savoured.

So the next time you look at yourself, count the Fs carefully. And never mind how many you can count the first time, remember there are many, many more.

Friends, family, faith and fun—these are just some of the things in our lives that our minds take for granted and get conditioned to miss out on.

Handling Pressure: The Irfan Pathan Way

When you are under pressure, what do you think of most?

The cause of the pressure, right? Under pressure, what does your mind focus on? Your shortcomings? Failures? When faced with the challenge of walking on a thin log across a stream, why can we think only of falling into the water?

We can all benefit from learning to put things in perspective, particularly when we are under pressure. There's a lesson to be learnt in this from Irfan Pathan, the Indian pace bowler who journeyed from poverty to superstardom to failure to survival to success . . . All in quick succession. How does he handle pressure? To find the answer, let's fly across to The Gabba in Brisbane.

It was the second final of the Commonwealth Bank Series 2008. India versus Australia. India had won the first game, and powered by yet another fabulous knock from Tendulkar (91 runs off 121 balls), India had posted a competitive 258 in 50 overs—a score that gave them a fighting chance of registering a rare series win against the world's number one team.

In reply, Australia didn't start too well. After a miserable score of 8 for 2, and then 32 for 3, the middle order led a spirited rally to take the game to the wire. With one over left, the equation was tantalizing—6 balls to go, 13 runs to get. And two wickets in hand.

Dhoni and the think tank deliberated on who should bowl the last over. India's pace spearhead, Sreesanth, had bowled well, totting up 2 for 43 from 9 overs, and looked the obvious candidate. Instead, the skipper threw the ball to Irfan.

Now, Irfan had had an ordinary day. Pretty much like the season itself—and questions were being asked about whether he truly deserved a place in the team. Irfan had proved to be the most expensive of India's bowlers in the game, his 6 overs yielding 51 runs. And no wickets. Not quite the figures that give you confidence to bowl the last and decisive over. Irfan was clearly a man under pressure.

If you are a cricket fan, you probably remember what happened next. First ball to James Hopes, batting on 60, looking like guiding Australia to a win . . . A single. Second ball: Irfan strikes and Nathan Bracken is gone, caught by Piyush Chawla in the deep. But luckily for

Australia, Hopes crosses over and takes strike. Four balls to go, 12 to get. Third ball: Hopes gets 2 runs. Now, 10 runs needed. Three balls to go. Fourth ball: Pathan strikes again. Hopes goes and, as commentators delighted in remarking that day, with that crashed Australia's 'Hopes'!

In the post-match interview, a TV reporter asked Irfan about the pressure he felt when he came on to bowl that last over. What was he thinking? Irfan's reply was revealing. He said that as he went up to bowl, he thought of his childhood, of the days when his father—a lowly paid *muezzin* in the local mosque—struggled to feed the family. He thought of the stress his parents went through trying to get his sister married. That he said was pressure. Real pressure. What did he have to do? Simple. Just bowl 6 balls and not give away 13 runs . . . Surely that's no pressure, he said to himself!

We could all learn from Irfan how to put things in perspective. Under pressure, it's easy to focus on the problem at hand, and feel burdened. Overwhelmed. We could instead think of how blessed we are, and think of the others who may not be as lucky. That would help take the mind away from the problem. Make it seem almost trivial. And help us perform to the best of our abilities.

Whatever the mind focuses on tends to grow. Think of your problems, and they will seem to grow bigger. Focus on your strengths, and they will seem to get magnified too. As always, the choice is yours.

When faced with the challenge of walking on a thin log across a stream, make sure your mind does not get filled with thoughts of falling into the water.

How Much Is Hundred Rupees?

In the days when everyone was talking about layoffs and zero bonuses and plunging stock markets, I was reminded of a story that encapsulates our tendency to behave somewhat irrationally when it comes to money.

Imagine that you are in a store, buying a watch. You like the brand and the design. The strap is just right, and at Rs 899, it fits your budget. You decide to pick it up but just as you are about to pay for it, you bump into a dear friend. He notices the watch and tells you that he's seen the same watch in the store across the road—priced at Rs 799. A whole hundred rupees lower!

What would you do? Most of us, I suspect, would walk across to the other store, and save hundred rupees. Why spend Rs 899 when you can get the same watch for Rs 799? Makes perfect sense.

Now, imagine another scenario. You are at a store buying an expensive Swiss watch. You like the brand, and the design. It's priced at Rs 247,900. And you decide to pick it up. Just as you are about to pay for it, you bump into a dear friend. He tells you that the same watch is available at a store across the road for Rs 247,800. A whole hundred rupees lower!

What would you do? Like most people, you would probably stay put and buy it there at the same store. After all, what's a hundred rupees when you are spending some 250,000 rupees?

It's quite strange actually. The truth is that the value of hundred rupees to an individual is—and should be—the same, independent of whether at that moment you are spending Rs 899 or Rs 247,900.

But we tend to get carried away by an unrelated metric. How much we are spending at a given moment affects our perception of the money being saved. If saving hundred rupees matters to you, it should matter to you independent of whether you are spending 1000 rupees or 100,000 rupees. We all need to learn to value the small stuff, those hundred-rupee notes, independent of how much we spend. In times of abundance, it's good to be cautious. It may just help stretch the abundance a bit.

Getting money to work for you is no different from getting people to work for you. If you don't treat your money (or your people) with respect, it (they) will leave you. And when the slowdown hits—as it inevitably will—those who valued those hundred rupees even while they were spending big, will find themselves better placed to tide over the difficult times.

I recall a powerful case study they taught at the Indian Institute of Management, Ahmedabad. It was the first class in the marketing elective taught by the late Professor Labdhi Bhandari. It was a one-page case involving two companies caught up in a price war. So what should the company do, asked the professor. What strategies should it adopt to stay competitive? Cut costs, came the reply from one of the students. And then, the classic response from Professor Bhandari: 'Cost cutting is not a strategy. It is an imperative. Don't wait for competition or for troubled times to launch cost-cutting initiatives. Cut costs at all times.'

Wise words those, which ring true to this day.

Clearly, it pays to value that hundred-rupee note. In times good and bad.

In times of abundance, it's good to be cautious. It may just help stretch the abundance a bit. If hundred rupees matters to you, it should matter to you independent of whether you are spending 1000 rupees or 100,000 rupees.

Of Balloons and People

A friend of mine runs a luxury car dealership in Coimbatore. He told me an interesting story about the salespeople in his showroom, and their instinctive responses when a customer walks in. They get excited when they see a well-dressed, seemingly affluent person walk into the store. Quick to sense a kill, all of them converge on him. They offer him coffee (and would the missus like a Pepsi?) and, since he seems to 'relate to them', the conversations tend to be long and animated.

However, when a seemingly regular guy, in a dhoti and a loose white shirt walks in, looking as if he parked his bicycle outside and is looking for directions, no one displays any interest. Why waste time—that's probably the thought playing on their minds. They let the watchman handle him and point him to the post office—if that's what he is looking for!

But here's the interesting bit. Years of minding the

store have taught my friend that, more likely than not, it is the ordinary-looking guy in the dhoti who will actually end up buying a car! He's probably got wads of currency notes stuffed into the pockets of his shorts, under his dhoti. The well-dressed, good-looking couple was probably just looking for an air-conditioned place to cool off a bit before heading back to some more window shopping!

Which is why, this is the first lesson my friend imparts to new members of his sales team: Never judge a customer by his appearance.

Years of mental conditioning have made us all think a bit like those salesmen. We tend to judge people by their external manifestations, the way they speak, the way they dress. Sure, first impressions are important but it's even more important to ensure that we don't get carried away.

Some of the smartest, brightest colleagues I have worked with have been shy and quiet and apparently easy to miss. No big talk, no fanfare. Just good minds, the willingness to work hard and a can-do attitude. The shirt is not always tucked in properly, the blue socks don't quite go well with the beige trousers, the heavy accent often jars. But hidden beneath all of that is a real treasure—a teammate you could bet your life on!

When I see young, ambitious people, I sometimes worry that they are quick to copy the mannerisms and styles and looks of their more successful role models—but don't spend as much time on developing the core: the real values that make for real success. They confuse the visible trappings of success with the real internal strengths that contribute to the success.

It probably says something about the world we live in that while we spend more on beauty treatments and clothes and cosmetics, we are reluctant to spend much on training ourselves, on opening our minds, on becoming better human beings. Young people often complain that the company is not spending enough on training them. They wait for the company to spend on their education. Yes, they pay for their own clothes, for that cool pair of sunglasses, for that monthly visit to the beauty salon. But training? 'That's not my responsibility' seems to be the refrain. Clearly, appearances seem to matter more to us than our core expertise and strengths.

I'm reminded here of the story of a balloon-seller at a village fair. Just the kind of fair made famous by Bollywood as the place where twin brothers get separated at the start of the movie, only to be reunited twenty years and sixteen reels later. Well, this balloon-seller was selling helium-filled balloons in various colours—red, blue, white, green, yellow . . .

The string of a red balloon snapped by accident and, as the balloon soared into the sky, the crowd roared and kids tugged at their parents' arms, urging them to get them balloons. Seeing that it was attracting attention, the balloon-seller released another balloon. This time, a blue one, that quickly soared towards the clouds. Soon after, he released a green balloon. Then a yellow one.

Seeing all the balloons going up, a little boy went up to the balloon-seller and innocently asked: 'If you release that white balloon, will it also soar as high as the rest?' The balloon-seller explained: 'Son, it's not the colour of the balloon that matters. It's what's inside that makes it rise!'

True of balloons. True of people too. Appearances don't matter. It's what is within that makes the difference. That's a lesson we would all do well to remember. When we look at other people. And when we look at ourselves. Look deeper. Look within.

It isn't the colour of the balloon that matters. It's what is inside it that makes it rise!

The Frog and the Scorpion

'I never thought he'd do this to me, not after all that I did for him!'

You must have heard this line before. Or perhaps, said it yourself. The sense of betrayal, of being let down, is gut-wrenching. And yet, it seems to recur with unfailing regularity. In offices. In relationships. In lives.

The sense of hurt seems to get compounded by the belief that we did so much for that person. The notion is that since we've done so much—for that boss, that colleague, that friend—we've bought out his right to do something that would hurt us.

A friend of mine went to work as the CEO of a business that had been built by a self-made man—a terrific entrepreneur notorious for his whiplash tongue, his short temper and his interfering nature. Well-meaning friends warned the CEO-designate about the challenges and risks a professional manager would face in working with such a promoter. But my friend believed that the promoter needed him—a professional—desperately and would, therefore, change his ways to ensure the CEO's survival. 'We've talked about it,' he said to his friends, 'and the promoter has promised me that there will be complete respect, and absolutely no interference.' Twelve months later, the CEO was gone. Reason? Yes, you got it. Whiplash tongue, short temper, interference.

Have you heard the story of the scorpion and the frog? Seems the scorpion wanted to cross the stream but since he couldn't swim, he went over to the frog and said, 'Why don't you let me ride on your back? I can't swim!'

'I can't possibly let you do that!' said the frog. 'You are a scorpion. You will sting me!'

'Oh, you stupid frog!' said the scorpion. 'I couldn't possibly do that because if I did, we would both drown!'

Sensing the logic, and seeing an opportunity to win bragging rights for having helped a scorpion across the water, the frog agreed. Well, when they were in the middle of the stream, the scorpion stung the frog. 'Why did you do that?' asked the frog, shocked, and quickly going down in the water. 'Because I am a scorpion!' came the reply, as both the frog and the scorpion drowned.

Good thing to remember. Just because you do a good deed to a scorpion, it doesn't mean that it will stop him from stinging you.

Scorpions are scorpions. They sting. Expecting otherwise will set you up for disappointment. Time and again.

Scorpions will be scorpions. They will sting.

Eat That Frog!

Given that perhaps the only thing that Mukesh Ambani and Bill Gates and you and I have in equal measure is the number of hours in our day, it probably makes sense for us to figure out how to manage time better! Time management is, not surprisingly, high on everyone's list of things to get better at.

One of the habits often recommended—and something that I have found useful too—is making a to-do list. It's a practice that has worked for me. I make a list of things to do, then go about striking them off as I accomplish them. And here's a little trick I have often used in the past to feel good: I throw in a few not-so-important but easy-to-finish tasks on the list. And then start to feel really good as I strike them off. Do you find yourself doing that too, and feeling suitably busy?

Here then is a piece of advice that could dramatically improve your productivity. It's powerful. And it's the title of a book by the self-help author Brian Tracy—*Eat That Frog!*

There's an old saying that if you woke up each morning and ate a live frog, you could probably spend the rest of the day content in the knowledge that nothing worse could happen. Think about that!

Now think of a frog as your most important task, your number one priority, the one most likely to make the greatest impact. Because it's a tough act, we keep pushing it away, hoping that perhaps it will go away on its own. It doesn't. Often, the most important task is also the toughest. It pays to get over it—first! Eat that frog, be done with it and the rest seems so easy then.

It stands to reason that if you have to eat that frog, it won't help to keep it in front of you and stare at it all day long. Yet, that's exactly what we tend to do. We keep that one big task, that big-impact tough call, hanging over our heads, which only increases our stress levels. We keep staring at the frog. We keep thinking of how ugly it is. We worry about the awful taste. And we hope that all of this will make the frog more palatable. Or better still, we hope the frog will go away. However, nothing changes. Your most important task remains to be done. The frog still needs to be eaten. Go ahead, serve yourself.

And yes, here's another tip. If you have to eat two frogs, eat the bigger, uglier one first. Prioritize. Make sure you do the more important task first.

The eat-that-frog philosophy is, ultimately, not just about managing time. It's perhaps good advice for managing life. In relationships and at work, it pays to grab the bull by its horns, forget the trivial bits and focus on the big-ticket items. They make the biggest difference. Talking about them, bitching, worrying, procrastinating, constantly looking at them—all these won't help at all. The benefit you would have gained from accomplishing your biggest task will remain elusive, and stress and worry levels will only mount.

Take the first step. Identify your frog. Your big task. Your big-impact action step. Your number one priority. Once you've done that, go ahead—eat that frog.

And taste the difference!

If you have to eat that frog, it doesn't help to stare at it all day long.

Making a Difference, the Starfish Way

In a memo to all company employees, a memo that found its way into the media, Infosys CEO Kris Gopalakrishnan urged each employee to save ten dollars. 'If each of us saves just ten dollars, the cumulative amount would be a million dollars!' he wrote. Sage advice that. Good for Infosys, good for any organization.

In a large company, it's tempting for an individual employee to see large spends all around him and wonder: 'What difference will my ten dollars make?' The cumulative effect, the real impact, is often hard to perceive. And that keeps us from taking that first step. Keeps us from saving the ten dollars we easily can.

It's like that with our rants against our elected political leaders too. We are angry with the leadership. We seek change. And yet, when election time comes around, we don't bother to vote. 'After all,' we argue, 'what difference does one vote make?' And so it goes on.

We don't bother too much about throwing litter from our cars on to the streets either. 'The city is so dirty. What difference will another empty packet of chips make?' And we don't bother writing that small cheque that could help educate a poor girl child somewhere. After all, illiteracy is a huge problem in India. Paying to educate one child won't alter the numbers, will it?

It's like that at work too. We see a big problem and, fazed by its enormity, we stop taking those small baby steps towards solving it.

At Pepsi, for instance, one of the challenges was to get glass-fronted Pepsi refrigerators in retail outlets to be pure—stocked only with Pepsi's range of soft drinks. (No Coke please, Pepsi is paying for the fridge!) Well, retailers across the country were inclined to use the refrigerators they received from any soft drink company to cool everything they stocked—competing soft drinks, water, *lassi*, even *paneer*! Imagine trying to remove all that stuff from millions of coolers across outlets, across the country. It was a daunting task, seemingly hopeless. But the message to the sales team was clear: When you visit an outlet, don't leave until you've made the Pepsi cooler pure. As salespeople questioned what difference one cooler would make in a country full of impure coolers, this story came in handy. The tale of the woman and the starfish.

An old man, walking on a beach one morning, noticed a young woman walking ahead of him. As she walked, she would bend down every now and then, picking up starfish and throwing them back into the sea. Catching up with the woman, he asked her why she was doing this. She replied that the poor starfish had got washed ashore at night, and would probably die in the morning sun.

'But this beach stretches for miles and there are probably a million starfish on the shore,' countered the old man. 'How will your effort make any difference?' The young woman looked at the starfish in her hand, flung it into the water and said, 'Well, it sure made a difference to that one.'

In our lives and careers, we regularly come across such starfish moments. Seemingly insurmountable problems. Where your individual contribution to the solution seems small, almost trivial. The next time that happens to you, your starfish moment, remember you could do one of two things. Either shrug your shoulders and say why bother, what difference can it make. Or take that small step and do your bit.

The beach may be long. There may be millions of starfish. But throwing one back means one life saved. You can make a difference!

Every little bit counts. Do your bit. Make a difference.

How Good Are You with Bad News?

Picture this. You are the CEO of a shipping company. Let's call it White Star Line Shipping Company. You and your team have been working on building the world's largest luxury passenger ship, with safety features that make it almost unsinkable. The world, including your shareholders and your board, is watching with bated breath, to see how the investment in this dream project will pay off.

On the appointed day, your dear baby sets sail. As it nears the end of its maiden voyage, you get this business update from your line managers: '700 happy passengers reached New York safe.'

As performance reports go, that's pretty darn accurate. But it doesn't quite tell the whole story. It doesn't tell you that this is the story of the *Titanic*. Your luxury liner just hit an iceberg, and 1517 people lost their lives. Only 706 survived, and just about made it to New York. Happy to be alive.

The corporate world is full of stories of the '700 passengers reached New York' kind. Given the pressures to perform, the quirky demands of quarterly earnings guidance, unforgiving boards and markets and, of course, fat bonuses tied in to results delivery, bad news is not only slow to come, it's often suppressed. Hidden and buried.

We either find newer metrics to report ('volume sales are lower, but in value terms we've grown') or we report anecdotal evidence ('who says people prefer our competitors' products? I have this email from a customer who raves about us') or we conveniently brush the past under the carpet of a rational excuse, and paint a rosy, dramatically different future ('we are down 30 per cent versus plan but with the monsoon behind us, we should be able to get to our targets for the year') . . .

It's not just the sales and marketing guys who succumb to the temptation of delaying the bad news. CEOs and boards are guilty too. Remember Bear Stearns, the iconic US investment bank that collapsed in 2008? On Monday, 10 March, the CEO Alan Schwartz was quoted as saying, 'Bear Stearns's balance sheet, liquidity and capital remain strong!' And by Sunday 16 March, the bank was dead and gone. As subsequent events on Wall Street have confirmed, the distance between a blue-chip investment bank and bankruptcy has now shrunk to just a weekend.

Friday's hero is Monday's basket case. Why didn't the CEOs of the errant banks sound the warning bells earlier? Why do sales managers delay bad news? Why do managers look to report imaginary silver linings in the face of otherwise gloomy, dark clouds?

The answer lies in our ability (or should that be inability?) to manage bad news—both in terms of delivering it and receiving it.

It has been well documented that for success in the corporate world, what managers need is not just a high IQ (intelligence quotient) but also a high EQ (emotional quotient). I'd like to add a new rider: The difference between good managers and truly great ones lies in their BNQ. Bad News Quotient. The ability to manage bad news. Both in terms of delivering it, and taking it in.

Senior managements and boards need to ensure that they create an environment where they get the bad news first. If you scream and shout when you hear the bad news, it's unlikely you'll get to hear very much more in the future. (A dear friend once recounted how her seventeen-year-old son, a sophomore in a prestigious American college, told her about his newly acquired blonde American girlfriend. As a mom, she was instantly nervous, disappointed, even angry but concealed her uneasiness and didn't say a word. 'I knew,' she said to me over lunch, 'that if I showed my displeasure, that would be the last time he'd tell me anything.')

It's fashionable, but grossly inadequate, to merely say: 'Give me the bad news first.' What matters is how you react thereafter. Often, too often, external pressures get cited and the bad news is wished away, the good news forcibly willed in. ('I am going to have none of it. Do whatever it takes, but you have to deliver the target profit.')

Similarly, when looking at dashboards and performance scorecards, it's important to have an agreed set of metrics to measure consistently. Else, managers get encouraged—nay, emboldened—to pick the isolated positive metric to report. A handkerchief-sized bit of good news is used to cover an entire body of failure. Spelling forecast as H-O-P-E is not just bad spelling—it's terrible business too!

Getting the bad news early not only helps prepare everybody for the impending disaster but, if delivered right and acted upon, it could actually help avert the disaster itself.

The next time you hear bad news and are ready to fly off the handle and demand that you want to hear none of it, pause. Check your own BNQ. How you receive the tiny bits of bad news determines whether the big bad news stories get delivered to you at all.

The next time you need to report bad news, muster the courage to deliver it. Straight up. Think of your BNQ. Your ability to manage bad news is perhaps a terrific measure of how good a manager you are.

That's not all. Once you get to work on building a team and an organization that's high on BNQ, you will find the culture spreads. Top to bottom. Chances are yours will be a more successful business, quickly reacting to the reality of the marketplace, making mid-course corrections, making the right moves. Fast.

And if that's not enough, you can be pretty sure too that in the unlikely event that your ship is sinking, you won't have to hear about 700 passengers reaching safe..

The difference between good managers and truly great managers lies in their BNQ, their Bad News Quotient. Their ability to manage bad news. Both in terms of delivering it, and receiving it.

VIII

WINNING WITH TEAMS

Flat-tyre Leadership

A friend of mine shared this wonderful story about Ratan N. Tata (RNT), the leader of the house of Tatas. The story may be apocryphal but it aptly sums up the genius of the man credited with transforming a somewhat sleepy giant into a global powerhouse. The man whose vision and dogged persistence brought the Nano to life.

One of RNT's first assignments was the stewardship of Nelco, the ailing electronics company in the Tata portfolio. The story goes that a team of Nelco's senior managers was driving to Nasik along with RNT. Halfway through, the car had a flat tyre. As the driver pulled up, all the occupants—including RNT—got off for a comfort break, leaving the driver to change the tyre.

Some of the managers welcomed the break; it allowed them the much-needed chance to light up cigarettes! Some used the opportunity to stretch, smile, share a joke. Then, one of them noticed that RNT was not to be seen, and wondered aloud where he might have vanished.

Was he behind a bush? Had he wandered off to the roadside dhaba for a quick cup of tea? Was he perhaps asking the owner about the brand of tea he used, and looking for feedback on Tata Tea? Or was he mingling with some passers-by, listening to their stories?

None of these, in fact.

While his colleagues were taking a break, RNT was busy helping the driver change the tyre. Sleeves rolled up, tie swatted away over the shoulder, hands expertly working the jack and spanner, bouncing the spare tyre to check if the tyre pressure was okay, droplets of sweat on the brow, a smile on his face . . .

In that moment, the managers accompanying RNT got a lesson in leadership they haven't forgotten. And that's a moment that the driver of that car probably hasn't forgotten either.

Great leaders are really all about this. Leading from the front. Rolling up their sleeves. Being one with the frontline colleagues who get the work done. And working as a team, with scant regard for hierarchy. And doing all this because they believe. Not because someone is watching.

Unfortunately, too many corporate leaders spend lifetimes waiting for that one big moment to arrive for them to demonstrate their leadership skills. That big competitive onslaught. That major crisis. That new product launch. The truth is that your true leadership style—your true colours—are probably most evident in ordinary everyday moments. Like that flat tyre. Such moments come up before leaders every day. Everywhere. How you treat each such moment is a terrific barometer of your leadership strength, a great indicator of how you will behave when the big moment of challenge really does arrive.

Many young managers tend to spend all their time trying to manage upwards—focusing their attentions and energies on the boss, rather than on their subordinates. In a sense, like the managers in the car that day, we all too tend to look for what our own RNT may be doing . . . Not for what the hapless chauffeur might be up to.

Over the past few decades, several of RNT's colleagues at the house of Tatas have been privileged to be a part of the unique 'flat-tyre' brand of leadership. They have been privy to several such magical moments.

Some years ago, RNT went public with his dream of creating a one-lakh-rupee car. Experts said it was impossible. Cynics laughed it off. And most seemed to agree that the great man had probably overreached himself.

But then, in a culmination of the dream—and in what became one of the finest symbols of the great Indian entrepreneurial spirit—RNT unleashed the Nano on an incredulous country. At a price tag of—yes, you guessed it right—one lakh rupees only. Nano's launch was in many senses the culmination of a dream shared by several people who worked shoulder to shoulder to make the impossible possible. Drivers, designers, shop-floor workmen, managers . . . and a fabulous leader. Against all odds, defying the experts, RNT and his team managed to do the impossible. As he put it, 'After all, a promise is a promise.'

Some years from now, as millions in India—and perhaps around the world—happily drive around in their oh-so-affordable Nanos, they may not know it . . . but one flat tyre probably started it all.

Great leaders lead from the front. Roll up their sleeves. Become one with the frontline colleagues who get the work done. They work as part of a team, with scant regard for hierarchy. And they do all this because they believe. Not because someone is watching.

Flying Kites; Managing Teams

One of my abiding childhood memories revolves around flying kites in Jaipur. To be able to fly a kite was to come of age, as it were, to become a big boy. As a six-year-old, it felt real cool to be able to get a kite to take off and soar into the skies.

I still remember the first time I managed to fly a kite, after several days of aborted take-offs. I remember how we'd wrap the string (or *manja*) around an empty tin of Cherry Blossom shoe polish. The right way to do it was to tie a knot, so the string would be secured at one end to the tin. But at six, while I was learning to fly a kite, I still hadn't learnt to tie a knot!

My heart filled with joy as the kite flew higher and higher. The joy soon turned to heartbreak, as the string slipped through my palms and the kite flew away . . . all because I hadn't knotted the other end to the tin. I was left with an empty tin of shoe polish in my hands, tears in my eyes.

That experience taught me a lesson and inculcated a streak of caution, a dash of prudence that has stayed with me ever since. It brought home the virtue of ensuring that the basics are right, always. The need to balance risk and reward. The need to blend caution and aggression. The need to ensure that the knot is tied before you set off to fly kites! To this date, when things are going well—too well—I worry that something might just go wrong. I feel a desperate urge to check if the string is tied to the tin of shoe polish!

While my love affair with kites waned as I grew up, the lessons from kite flying continued. My next kite-flying lesson was thanks to the movies.

Remember *Namak Haraam*? That fabulous movie of the 1970s starring the two superstars Rajesh Khanna and Amitabh Bachchan? While opinion was divided about which of the two stole the show, my favourite character in the movie was a drunk poet-cum-kite-seller, played by Raza Murad.

There is a particularly poignant scene when the drunk poet is about to die. He says something that has stayed with me ever since—sort of a guiding philosophy in my life. As he sees his end drawing near, the kite-seller looks at all the kites in his store and spells out his last wish. 'When I die,' he says to a friend, 'distribute all these kites among the little kids in the slums. Let them fly the kites, so that everybody watching the kites soaring in the skies will know that the strings that control the guys on top are in the hands of the little fellows on the ground!' (*'Ooper waalon ki dor neeche waalon ke haathon mein hoti hain!'*)

A powerful lesson when it comes to dealing with people and teams. Humility works, like magic. And it's good to understand that when you have people working under you, or for you, you depend on them far more than you realize. You might think you are in control, that you are the boss, when the reality is quite the opposite. Whether it's your secretary or your sales team—just about anyone who works for you—it's good to remember the lesson from the kites! You are only as good as the team that's supporting you.

We see this lesson in sport too. Captains are only as good as their teams. The real power lies in the hands of individual performers. When a captain starts to think that he makes the difference—that he wields the power—that is usually the beginning of the end. Just recognizing the role of frontliners is often a great first step towards watching them soar in the skies.

The similarity between teams and kites doesn't end here. If you've ever flown a kite, you would have noticed that if you want it to fly farther and higher, you don't push it. You pull it. To make a kite fly higher, you need to pull it towards you.

People are like that too. Push them, and they usually won't perform. Push them harder, and they will probably fall apart. As will you. But pull them towards you, show them you care, and watch them fly. Believe me, it works. With kites. And with people.

Perhaps organizations should consider celebrating Makar Sankranti, the festival of kites (14 January) as the Day of the Frontliner. A day to honour the foot soldiers who actually make our world go round. The salesmen and the accounting staff and the folks in administration—unsung heroes who all make a difference. Recognize them. Thank them. And get reminded of some key lessons in life . . . The folks down there usually hold the strings to all those guys on top. If you want people to fly higher, don't push them. Pull them towards you. And watch them take off!

And while you are at it, as you take pleasure in watching your kite soar, it might also be a good idea to check and ensure that you have tied the string to your tin of shoe polish.

To make a kite fly higher, you need to pull it towards you. Not push it. People are like that too.

Of Sales Teams and Remote Controls

It was the summer of 1987. The battlefield: Andhra Pradesh. The war: Rin versus Nirma. At stake: Market share leadership in India's largest detergent bar market.

Rin was the blockbuster brand of Hindustan Lever, now Hindustan Unilever. Rin was the undisputed market leader. The brand immortalized by some of the most memorable advertising campaigns of that time. Remember the tagline: '*Bhala uski kameez meri kameez se safed kaise?*' ('How is his shirt whiter than mine?') And remember how the non-Rin guy always missed the bus?

But away from the hallowed portals of Lever House in Mumbai, a silent revolution was gathering momentum in the marketplace. A low-priced, value-for-money yellow detergent bar was rapidly making inroads into the market and putting pressure on Rin's sales graph. Offering more (20 per cent extra) for less (almost 50 per cent off on the price of the market leader), the Nirma bar was changing the rules of the game.

As Rin sales plummeted and sales teams found themselves falling short of their targets month after month, the pressure mounted. Understandably so. After all, Rin was the top profit grosser for the company. So when Rin sneezed, Hindustan Lever caught a cold.

Brand managers unleashed attractive deep-discount trade schemes to load up the retailer. These schemes had worked well for several years but in the face of the Nirma onslaught, retailers didn't quite bite the extra discount. Sales continued to dip.

Innovative, attractive sales force contests were organized to reward the stars in Lever's galaxy of salespeople. In the past, legends were created when several salespeople would beat their targets by a mile, to win not just a few grams of gold or a holiday trip but honour and glory. Against the Nirma juggernaut, however, that didn't work either. Rin shares continued to slide.

More pressure was placed on the sales team. The quality of execution was questioned. Experienced, star salespeople found themselves put on the mat. Distributors found themselves saddled with increasing inventory and, under the pressure, the entire distribution system started to crack up.

Instead of rethinking the brand strategy or revisiting the marketing mix, and responding smartly to the changed competitive scenario, the spotlight stayed on the hapless sales system. 'It has delivered all these years, so why not now?' was the refrain.

Seems the thinking in headquarters was somewhat like this: 'The sales guys have just gotten lazy. Let's put some pressure, let's crack the whip, results will follow . . .'

If you think about it, we are all like that. When things go wrong—as they often do—we blame execution. We blame people. We increase pressure. But to no avail.

Our approach in such situations is akin to the way we handle the TV remote. Want to switch channels, zap that ad, mute that irritant judge on a reality show? Press a button on your remote. And it works!

And that goes on for months. Press button. Change channel. Adjust volume. Whatever.

But one day, the channel does not change. So what do we do? Press the button harder. Point it in the TV's direction. Move closer to the screen. Slam the remote. Hit it against the palm. Hard. Harder. Everyone becomes a remote expert, and takes a shot at pressing the buttons. 'It worked yesterday, no reason why it shouldn't today' . . . goes the thinking.

As we press harder, we increase the wear. The hapless remote gives up and calls it quits. All this when perhaps all we needed to do was change the battery.

It's like that with sales teams too. When targets are missed, the sales system comes under pressure. If you press harder, they will crack up. And leave.

The next time you find your star sales team missing targets regularly, pause for a while before pressing the buttons harder. Perhaps it's time to question your strategy. Time to change the batteries as it were. Like Hindustan Lever finally did. They unleashed a new brand, Wheel detergent bar, at a lower price point, to take Nirma head-on. Both Rin and Wheel flourished. The Nirma juggernaut was halted.

And the Lever folks lived happily ever after!

If the TV channel doesn't change when you press the button on your faithful remote, what do you do? Press harder. Slam the remote. Hit it against the palm. All this, when all you need to do really is change the batteries. It's like that with teams too.

Lessons for the New Leader

What happens when an organization gets a new CEO from outside? What's it like when a sales team gets a new manager hired from another organization? When the Indian cricket team gets a foreign coach, why does it work on some occasions and bomb on others?

It all boils down to the attitude of the new leader. There's enough research to show that the first 100 days are critical for a new leader, in any such situation. The first few steps, the early interactions with the team, the initial impact and the overall chemistry between the leader and his team in the early days often define the long-term success—or failure—of that engagement. How should a new leader approach such an assignment?

Well, he could learn a lesson or two from Dastur Neryosang Dhaval, the leader of the first group of Zoroastrians that came into India. It all happened in AD 755 in the small town in Gujarat called Sanjan. About five hundred Parsi families landed on Indian shores, having fled from Persia. They reached Sanjan, a prosperous little town ruled by a benevolent Hindu king called Jadi Rana. Dastur, the chief of the Parsis, went to the king's court to request him for refuge. Being somewhat apprehensive of the tall, fair warrior-like tribe and unsure of his little kingdom's ability to absorb and provide for the immigrants, the king called for a bowl of milk, filled to the brim. He showed it to the Parsi chief, to symbolize the fact that the kingdom was full. There was no room for more people!

But Dastur was not about to give up so easily. He asked one of the attendants to get him some sugar. He took a spoonful of the sugar and mixed it in the bowl, letting it dissolve—signifying that the Zoroastrians would mingle with the people in Sanjan and sweeten their lives. Impressed, the king allowed the Parsis to settle in his kingdom. The rest, as they say, is history.

Several valuable lessons in leadership flow from that bowl of milk and sugar.

First, leaders moving into a new team or organization must remember that, in most cases, the bowl is almost always perceived to be full to the brim. The view in the team often is this: 'We are doing fine by ourselves . . . We don't really need a new leader . . .' Remember, it's got nothing to do with the way the team is or with who you are. The organization always sees itself as a full-to-the-brim cup when a new leader arrives.

Second, like the sugar itself, leaders must learn to mingle with the team and be willing to let their identity, and their ego, become subservient to the needs of the team. After all, once the sugar dissolves in the team, you want people to exclaim how sweet the milk is. No one's going to be talking about how good the sugar was. Yet, many new leaders focus more on being recognized as great leaders—good sugar—rather than on impacting teams and creating a fabulous organization (sweet milk)!

Third, it also helps to remember that once the sugar dissolves in the milk, it sweetens the last drop of milk. The sugar's impact is not confined merely to the drops of milk that come in direct contact with it. Leaders must aim to impact the man in the frontline, the soldier at the battlefront, the last drop, not just the coterie of direct reports in the corridor leading up to the corner room.

Finally, it's most important to understand and appreciate what's inside the bowl. Is it milk? Or water? Or soda? Understanding the people and the organization has to be the first step in the leader's journey.

It's also good to remember the advice from Marshall Goldsmith, the man who helps successful leaders get even better: What got you here won't get you there. You may have built your reputation and career with a certain style (aggressive, task oriented) but your new role—and the new team or organization—might require a different approach. Young managers are like slices of lime. Early in their career, these slices of lime make instant impact. A few drops of lime turn soda into lemonade, make bland rice interesting and turn carrots and cucumber into delicious salad. As a reward, the manager moves up into a new role. A new organization. What awaits them here? A bowl full of milk. And we all know what happens when you squeeze a lime into a bowl of milk!

Good leaders make sure that their armoury includes equal quantities of sugar and lime. And, more important, they make sure they first understand the organization and then decide on what would work best!

Every organization sees itself as a full-to-the-brim cup when a new leader arrives. Like sugar in a cup of milk, leaders must learn to mingle with the team and be willing to let their ego become subservient to the needs of the team. Once the sugar dissolves in the milk, you want people to exclaim how sweet the milk is. Not how good the sugar was.

Catching Fish with Strawberries and Cream

One of the more popular pastimes at home these days is playing Taboo, a popular word-guessing game. It's simple and it's fun. The object of Taboo is for you to get your partner to guess the word (or phrase) mentioned on your card, without using that word—or five other words—mentioned on the card.

Here's what I find fascinating. Often, very often, you come across a word that seems oh-so-simple. And you come up with what you think is the perfect clue, but your partner struggles to get it. It seems so easy to you and you think your clueing is bang on, so how come she isn't guessing it. And instead of changing tracks and trying something else, you get frustrated, you show your anger and that makes your partner more nervous. And she doesn't get it at all.

Like it happened one night. The phrase I had was

'private equity'. And I said ICICI Venture. (After all, they were the PE investors in the company I worked with then.) And my daughter responded with words like 'owners', 'boss', 'Renuka', 'investor'—everything else, except private equity. And instead of just splitting it into two, and getting her to guess equity and private (pretty darn easy, I suspect), I got locked into the ICICI Venture idea. With scant regard for the fact that my daughter might just not relate to them as private equity.

This happens to all of us, often. We get caught up in our own thoughts and expect the others to see the world through our eyes. It seldom happens. And when they can't get it, we get angry. We get frustrated. And we lose the plot.

While recruiting young salespeople, we tell them about the fabulous car scheme they'd be eligible for as managers, and generous superannuation schemes. As if they care. All the poor guy is worried about is how much cash he'll take home at the end of the month.

We also force our likes (and dislikes) on to others. I once suggested to my wife: 'I have a fabulous idea for a romantic Sunday. Let's watch the India–Australia game.' Then I wondered through the rest of the day why she didn't quite seem excited!

That old master at winning friends and influencing people, Dale Carnegie, tells this powerful little story: 'I often went fishing up in Maine during the summer.

Personally, I am very fond of strawberries and cream, but I have found that for some strange reason, fish prefer worms. So when I went fishing, I didn't think about what I wanted. I thought about what they wanted. I didn't bait the hook with strawberries and cream. Rather, I dangled a worm or a grasshopper in front of the fish and said "Wouldn't you like to have that?"'

But we often go through our lives dangling strawberries and cream, wondering why the fish aren't biting. And instead of switching to what might work, we try and push the bowl of strawberries and cream even harder. Make the bowl larger, more attractive. Add a topping . . . All to no avail. And when the fish don't respond, we get frustrated. We scream. We shout. And we scare the fish away.

Successful leaders understand the need to look at things from the other's perspective. They seek to understand what turns others on. And then get to work on those levers. Not on what their personal outlook or passion might be. They also understand that while the worms will get the fish, if you go rabbit hunting, the worms won't work. Different people have different needs. And understanding their needs is the key to success.

The next time you find a teammate not quite warming up to your brilliant idea, pause. Swap the strawberries and cream for some smelly, squiggly worms. The next time you find yourself shaking your head in frustration at a teammate's indifference to your goals and your targets, relax. The problem is not with the fish. It's probably got to do with the fisherman putting strawberries and cream on the line!

It doesn't matter that you like strawberries and cream. To catch fish, you need to feed them worms. Not strawberries and cream!

The *Dahi Handi* Way!

Mumbai celebrates Janmashtami, the festival to commemorate the birth of Lord Krishna, in the '*dahi handi* way'. Legend has it that little Krishna was extremely fond of butter and would keep stealing it from the kitchen. His mother reacted by storing the butter (or yogurt) in a pot suspended high above the ground, out of her son's reach. But Krishna, smart kid that he was, would round up his friends, form a human pyramid and climb up to reach the butter!

Even now, across localities in Mumbai, Janmashtami sees a re-enactment of Krishna's attempt to form a pyramid and get to the pot of yogurt—the dahi handi. All over town, pots filled with yogurt are suspended about twenty to thirty feet off the ground. Teams of enthusiasts—popularly known as Govindas—go around the city and form human pyramids to get to the pots. There are prizes to be won—and some of the tougher dahi handis offer cash prizes going up to lakhs!

Adding to the fun—and the challenge—is the fact that residents in the neighbouring apartments throw buckets of water on the group trying to form a pyramid, making it a wee bit more slippery—and tougher to get to the prize. Accidents happen too, and some falling pyramids are known to have resulted in broken bones.

Once, as we drove around watching the festivities and imbibing the competitive spirit amidst the strains of *Govinda ala re*, it struck me that the dahi handi is not just a celebration of Krishna's childhood antics but actually a celebration of teamwork. Mumbai's streets and the Govindas' pyramids offer several valuable life lessons they don't teach you in any B-school.

Here are some lessons from the Dahi Handi School!

1. **It takes all sorts to make a team.** Not all members of a team of Govindas are alike. There are some supremely athletic types who can climb on to other people's shoulders in a jiffy. Then there are the overweight types, who too play a solid role in creating a strong base for the pyramid. A team made up of lean athletic types alone might look good on paper but would probably not be as strong as a team with a mix of different body types—to play different roles.

Complementary skills make for winning teams. Diversity helps!

2. **The higher the pot, the bigger the prize.** There are some

easy-to-get pots, where a two-level pyramid (with perhaps a child perched atop a shoulder) can get the team a few thousand rupees. Then there is the almost six-storey-high dahi handi, which takes a nine-layer pyramid—and then some—to crack the pot. And the prize: Rs 1,111,011!

The difference mirrors a reality of life: The tougher the challenge, the greater the payoff.

3. **It's the challenge that drives the spirit of achievement.** When we saw a bunch of people falling off one particular pyramid, my wife instantly remarked in anguish, 'Why don't they spread mattresses on the ground to ensure that people don't get hurt when they fall?' Well, one of the drivers of top performance is the fear factor. What if I fail? What if I fall? It's this edge, or this feeling of walking on the edge, that often inspires us to do the extra bit, to take on the odds and deliver. Take away the fear, the challenge, and you take away the desire to achieve.

Truth is, life's tough. If you fall, you get hurt. No mattresses cushion your fall. Success lies in ensuring that when you fall, you quickly pick yourself up, dust your elbows and get right back to work. Just like the Govindas.

4. **What you achieve is determined by how high you set your sights.** Teams train and practise to reach a predetermined height. Some teams plan to make a three-level pyramid, for instance. If the pot is suspended beyond that height and requires an extra level, they just walk

away to the next pot. They've set their sights on pots that can be reached with three levels of the pyramid. Anything above that is out of bounds.

Our lives are like that too. What we achieve is determined largely by what we plan to achieve. Some goals may look more attractive but it helps to know your limitations, and play to a plan.

5. **Others will try to spoil your plans and make the road seem difficult.** It is symbolic that people watching from the comfort of their homes throw buckets of water on the Govindas. The trick in the pyramid—and in life, indeed—is to stay focused, not get fazed by detractors.

Be prepared for critics, for spoilers, for roadblocks.

6. **You should be proud to be part of a team!** The Govindas are regular men who labour through the rest of the year on mundane, often physically taxing jobs. But on the dahi handi day, they use some old-fashioned team-building tricks to create the winning magic. They all wear team colours (no fancy attire, just red vests for instance). They give their team a name, an identity, and make sure it is emblazoned across their chests, preferably over their hearts. They travel together. They eat together. There are no hierarchies. The man at the top of the pyramid is no different—and no more important—than the several men at the bottom. And they all have fun while they are at it!

Passion and teamwork can turn a bunch of ordinary folks into an unbeatable, winning team!

7. **You may be higher up but don't forget the shoulders you stand on.** The pyramid becomes possible because there are people who are willing to stay on the ground and allow others to climb on to their shoulders. They carry the load. They are the enablers. While all eyes are fixed on the man at the top, to see if he can reach the pot, spare a thought for the guys at the bottom who make it happen. And remember, if they all clamoured to be the man at the top, there would be no pyramid, no team, no reward.

Never forget the frontliners and the foot soldiers. They make the real difference!

8. **You gotta get your target.** When a team manages to break a pot, it wins the prize. But if it fails to break the pot, it gets nothing. Zilch. Whether you fall short by a whisker or by a mile, it makes no difference. Not getting to the target equals failure, never mind whether you came close or gave up without trying. That's the kind of target consciousness any leader would like to infuse in his or her team. Often, far too often, teams confuse effort with achievement, and expect rewards for coming close to achieving their targets.

Break pot, get prize. No pot, no prize! You have to demonstrate results.

9. **If you only go where others have gone, the pot is already taken.** The interesting bit about each dahi handi is that there is only one pot at any location. Once it's broken, it's all over. So if your team is following another winning team's tracks, you will get nothing. Wherever you go, you'll find that the prize is already taken!

Learn to go where no one else has been. Chart your own course. As Bob Dylan wrote, 'Don't be afraid not to follow the herd/Because where the herd's gone, the food is already eaten!'

10. **Finally, never mind how high the pot is, you just can't get there alone.** The dahi handi symbolizes your life goals—money, relationships, projects, happiness, fame, whatever. But the message is clear: Never mind what your goal is, you need a team to achieve it. You need other people. You need support.

Lone rangers may make good film heroes. In real life, teams win. If you can't work with a team, your goals will probably remain elusive. Think about it!

Never mind what your goal is, you need a team to achieve it. You need other people. Teamwork works. Always!

IX

OTHER PEOPLE

The Twenty-one People on a Football Field

You've probably heard of Professor Randy Pausch and his book, *The Last Lecture*. Randy was a professor of computer science at Carnegie Mellon University, which hosted a rather innovative series of lectures called, well, 'The Last Lecture'. They invited a professor to spend sixty minutes or so talking to students, imagining that it was his or her last lecture, ever. If they knew it was their last lecture, what would they tell their students? What messages would they want to convey before they vanished from the face of the earth? Professor Pausch was invited to deliver this lecture in September 2007.

There was one small difference, though. He didn't have to *imagine* that it was his last lecture. He had been diagnosed with pancreatic cancer and the doctors realistically gave him only about six more months to live. It was, in fact, his last lecture. Literally speaking. (Randy Pausch passed away in July 2008.)

It turned out to be quite an amazing lecture, delivered to a packed classroom, and subsequently went on to become one of the most viewed videos on YouTube. Randy titled his talk 'Really Achieving Your Childhood Dreams' and it was all about him dreaming big dreams as a child and then working to make them come true. It was laced with humour, poignancy and brilliance. It brought smiles to the faces of those present and tears to their eyes—simultaneously.

Randy revealed that he had always nurtured the dream of becoming an NFL footballer. In fact, my favourite little story from Professor Pausch's life concerns his first football coaching lesson.

It was the first day of football practice in school. All the kids were very excited and eagerly looking forward to their date with the school team coach. As the tall, well-built coach walked up to join them, the sense of excitement only increased. All eyes were on the coach but there was also a growing sense of unease as the students noticed that something was missing. The coach had come but he hadn't brought along a football! One brave kid ventured to ask the coach about the missing football.

In response, the coach surveyed his brood and asked: 'How many players on a football field?'

'Twenty-two,' was the response.

'And how many footballs on a football field?'

'One!' yelled the kids, in unison.

'Right,' said the coach. 'At any point in time, only one man has the ball. Today, we are going to learn what the other twenty-one people on the field do then.'

That's a great lesson in how teams work! Life is, in many ways, like a game of football. While all eyes are usually on the man with the ball, it's the other twenty-one people who really make the difference. While people admire the individual dribbling skills of a footballer, it's important to know that games are won by teams that play as teams. If every individual just tried to control the ball all the time, the team would almost certainly never win.

Also, at times, the biggest factor in a team's success comes from the contribution and support of players who are not the cynosure of all eyes. Not the guys with the ball. Think about it.

The next time you talk to your team, remember that the 'other twenty-one' guys make a difference too! Don't get too caught up with retaining possession of the ball. Remember, your role too could be as one of those twenty-one others, in making a difference.

Life is not only about what you do when you have the ball—it's about what you do when someone else has the ball.

Charlie Plumb and the Parachute Packer

Charlie Plumb is an incredible guy. A decorated US war veteran, a navy fighter pilot. And a fabulous example of the indomitable human spirit. You may not have heard of him but he is just the kind of hero we all probably fantasized about as little kids. And his life story makes for a fascinating read.

He flew the F-4 Phantom fighter aircraft on seventy-four successful combat missions over North Vietnam. With five days to go to his return home, on his 75th mission, disaster struck. His plane was shot down. Luckily, Captain Plumb managed to eject from the aircraft and activate his parachute. That saved his life. Unluckily for him, he was captured and jailed, confined to a tiny cell—8 feet by 8 feet. He spent the next 2103 days—that's six long years—being tortured and humiliated as a prisoner of war before he could finally return home.

Charlie now spends his time sharing his story with others, helping people discover the strengths they need to tap into to overcome challenges in their own lives. He talks of the fear and the loneliness, the stench emanating from the bucket that served as his toilet, the darkness and the gloom in his cell. And he talks of surviving, of not letting the spirit take a beating, of never giving up.

But my favourite Charlie Plumb story is set in happier times. It's not about the six years of misery in a Vietnam jail but about a calm evening in a restaurant in Kansas City, several years later. Charlie was enjoying his meal when he noticed a gentleman seated a few tables away. He had to notice him. The gentleman was staring at him.

Charlie didn't think much of it until, a few minutes later, the man walked up to him and said: 'You're Charlie Plumb?'

'Yes,' replied Captain Plumb, standing up and extending his hand in greeting.

'You flew jet fighters in Vietnam. You were on the aircraft carrier Kitty Hawk. You were shot down. You parachuted into enemy hands and spent six years as a prisoner of war,' continued the stranger.

'How in the world do you know all that?' asked Captain Plumb.

He replied, 'I was the guy who packed your parachute.'

Captain Plumb was left quite speechless, a sense of

shock mixed with awe, even as the man continued with a twinkle in his eye, 'I guess it worked!'

Captain Plumb thanked the man again, and again, and before parting, he couldn't help asking: 'Do you remember all the parachutes you packed?'

'Not quite,' came the reply. 'It's enough for me just to know that I have served.'

Later that night, as Captain Plumb tossed about in his bed, his mind flashed back to his days as a fighter pilot. He wondered how many times he may have passed by the 'parachute packer' without even acknowledging his presence. He wondered if he ever said 'Good morning!' or 'How are you?' to the man. After all, Captain Plumb was a fighter pilot and the other guy was just a sailor. He couldn't have cared less.

We may not all be fighter pilots but we all have our parachute packers. People who build our safety nets, encourage us and, in their own small ways, make our successes possible. They remain unsung but somewhere inside, you know they made a difference. It could be that teacher from primary school, that salesman in a faraway town, that workman in the factory, that super-efficient secretary or that accounts clerk who always seemed to have the information you urgently needed . . . Through life's challenges, through the take-offs and crash landings in your career and life, they were the people who made it all possible. When the going got tough, they kept you going. They just did their jobs—but boy, they sure made you look good. Who do you turn to when the chips are down? So who is packing your parachute?

Unlike Captain Plumb, we aren't always fortunate enough to come face to face with our parachute packers. So we often don't get the chance to say thank you. Good idea then to think of the parachute packers in your life, and pick up the phone to thank them. Today. Now.

More important, it's also a good idea to ask the question: Whose parachute are you packing? Who are the people you provide strength and encouragement to? Which people will put your name in the list of folks who made a difference to their lives? Real success and happiness often emerge not from the personal glory of winning but from the joy of having helped someone else win. Making a difference to someone—that's really what makes the difference in life. Time to practise your parachute-packing skills!

And finally, it's hard to miss a trait in Charlie Plumb that's the hallmark of all great leaders. In their biggest triumphs and greatest victories, they always, always turn the spotlight on to the unsung heroes. The ordinary folks who made a difference. The parachute packers.

The next time you are basking in glory, celebrating a record year or popping the champagne to mark a smashing new success, do spare a thought for your parachute packer.

Who is your parachute packer? More important, whose parachute are you packing?

The Great Wall of China

Historical monuments often tell fascinating tales. The Great Wall of China is no exception.

One of the world's seven wonders, the Great Wall was built (and rebuilt and re-rebuilt) between the fifth century BC and the sixteenth century AD. Stretching over 6400 km, the brick-and-mud structure was originally built to protect the northern boundaries of the Chinese empire from attacks by enemies, specifically the Mongolian and Xiongnu armies. No effort or expense was spared, and it did take an enormous amount of time, effort, money—and stone and mud and sweat and toil—to build the Great Wall.

Apparently two million people lost their lives in the mammoth project. The wall was strong enough to survive any onslaught from swords and spears—common weapons of the time. It was high enough to prevent soldiers from scaling it and climbing over into the Chinese empire. And it stretched long and far enough, making it virtually impossible for anyone to go around. For good measure, there were over a million guards manning the Great Wall. Quite a fortress, you'll agree. And almost impossible to penetrate.

So, did the Great Wall keep invaders at bay? Not quite. Successive armies got past it, and invaded the empire. In its first hundred years, there were three invasions, and history was witness to several more instances of armies quite easily penetrating the seemingly impossible-to-penetrate wall. After each attack, the wall was reinforced. More planning, more brick, more mud, more money spent. All to no avail. So what really happened?

It turns out that while they spared no effort or expense in building the wall, the rulers completely ignored the guards. These men were completely demotivated, very lonely and totally unhappy. They resented their rulers for punishing them with postings in such faraway places. And they just could not identify with the larger goal that the wall was built for.

So each time attackers came along, all they had to do was bribe the guards, and they would be happily waved in! The wall did not have to be penetrated; it was breached via a breach of trust! The Great Wall failed to meet its objective because the builders forgot to take the people along.

It's the same in organizations too. Failing to take people

along can render your best investments futile. Often, we pay too much attention to building the system and the process but don't bother about getting the support and involvement of the people who will make it happen. That's a recipe for disaster.

Consider, for instance, an organization trying to implement a new enterprise resource planning (ERP) package. It hires the best consultants, purchases the best software, upgrades the hardware . . . But, as any ERP implementer will tell you, the single most vital reason for failure is the lack of buy-in from the people within the organization. Building an internal task force, regular training of all users, creating process owners and preparing the organization for change—all these are important for successful ERP implementation. Almost as important as choosing the right package!

If you're responsible for a team, the lesson from the Great Wall is a good one to remember. Look at what happened to Kolkata Knight Riders in the Indian Premier League. They had John Buchanan, arguably one of the world's best coaches, supported by a nine-man army of experts. John built out a grand vision for a winning team, with multiple captains and newfangled theories. The team spent a lot of time acclimatizing to alien conditions, even ran a talent hunt in the run-up to the main event. But what of the team itself? No attention was paid to their desires or motivations. As a result, they felt alienated and insecure. No wonder then that KKR came a cropper in IPL Season 2. Clearly the guards didn't have their hearts in the game.

Several consumer goods companies have learnt this too. When they have a great new product backed by a powerful, big-budget marketing campaign, what do they do? Do they just launch the brand and then expect the consumers to come flocking in, swayed by the powerful advertising? No!

They recognize the role of the guards! A launch conference for the frontline is an integral part of the marketer's armoury. Getting the sales army to know the product, making them feel excited about the new launch is often critical to the success of the brand. It then percolates right down to the small-town distributor's salesmen. Getting him to wear a new T-shirt with the brand emblazoned on it, rewarding him for meeting launch targets—these are small but significant steps in ensuring that all the money spent on developing the new brand and the new marketing campaign does not go to waste.

Too often, organizations focus all their attention on building the Great Wall and pay scant attention to the guards manning the wall. That's an invitation to failure. Successful leaders and organizations realize that it's not enough to build the Great Wall—it's important to have the guards on your side too!

It's not about the structure or the system or the processes or the infrastructure. It's about the people, always about the people.

The Chairman's Questions

As a young sales manager peddling soap in Tamil Nadu, one of my fondest memories is of the first time the company chairman visited my market. It happened several years ago, but it taught me a lesson that's stayed with me, until this day.

A 'chairman's visit' was rather special and a lot of preparation went into ensuring it would go off well. The route was marked out, the markets identified, the distributors en route briefed. As the man who'd get to travel with the chairman, I was working hard to ensure I had answers to all the questions that might get thrown at me during the long drive. How were the brands performing? What were the growth rates? How was the competition behaving? How much money were we spending on local marketing? What was the profitability of the local distributor? I had the answers to all of these—and then some. What was the main crop in the region? What was the hardness of water in the area? What was the population? What percentage of villages was electrified? What was the main source of livelihood? The list seemed endless. But I was hopeful I would be up to it.

The appointed day arrived. The branch manager and I picked up the chairman at the airport and drove out to a small town, some 90 km outside Chennai. The initial discussions were rather general, and extremely friendly. He asked after my family, my education, my interests but an hour into the ride, I was still waiting for the real questions. As we crossed a paddy field, I was tempted to remark about the rainfall being almost 95 per cent of average this year, and how the yield per acre had improved by 20 per cent in the last decade. But I held myself back.

We reached the distributor's godown. After introductions and a quick review of his business, and the customary biscuits and *kaapi*, we were all set to go into the local market. As the salesman and the delivery boy stood outside, waiting for us expectantly, the chairman looked at me and asked the first real question:

'What's the name of that delivery boy?'

I had no clue! Now, in the scheme of things, the delivery boy was just a helper, an odd-job man who would deliver the boxes of soap and detergent ordered by the retailer. He'd lift the boxes on his shoulder and ferry them from the van to the shop. And he'd also stick posters on the shop's walls. That's all.

I knew the name of the distributor. I also knew his

prosperous moneylender's father's name. And I knew the name of the salesman. As a matter of fact, I had even learnt the district collector's name, just in case. But the delivery boy's name? I had no idea!

'I don't know. Is there a problem? Did he do something wrong?' I asked in reply.

The response was quick. 'No. I just want you to remember that each of these people makes a difference. And it's our job to know them, to acknowledge them. If you knew him by his name, and if you called it out, he'd feel special. You could make his day. And he'll do everything he can to help you meet your goals. We all tend to ignore these people even though they spend all their lives working for us, without asking for or expecting anything in return. They are our real heroes. I want you to remember that.'

I may not have realized it then but, in that moment, I had received a master class. On leadership. On success. And on managing people. A lesson I haven't forgotten. Knowing your own team and acknowledging their contribution are far more important than knowing your sales numbers—or the names of 'people who matter'.

In our lives, we tend to look up all the time, at our superiors. We seldom find time for those 'lowly folks' who are looking up at us. The peon, the security guy, the office assistant, that delivery boy—all of them play roles in helping us succeed.

The next time you come across one of your 'delivery boys', do remember to acknowledge his presence. It might just be a smiling nod or a hand on his shoulder but remember, it can change his life. And yours too.

We tend to worry about the seemingly big stuff—sales growth, market shares, profitability. But we forget the small stuff—the people who help make it happen. The foot soldiers. And we forget that in their own way, they impact all of these. Good idea to remember that.

To tell the true character of a person, you don't need fancy psychometric tests or long months of behavioural assessments. Just observe how he behaves with ordinary folks—the lift operator, the driver, the office peon, the waiter in a restaurant. Does he scream and shout and show who the boss is? Or does he say thank you as he walks out of the elevator? Is he rude? Or does he speak with respect, and with a smile? The answers can be revealing.

In our constant quest to look up and please our bosses, we keep hoping he remembers our name and acknowledges our role. We love it when that happens. And yet when it is our turn to acknowledge those who work for us, we are often found wanting. During that visit several years ago, I was perhaps just another 'delivery boy' for the chairman of India's largest consumer goods company but, by taking interest in me and getting to know me—and making sure I did the same with my 'delivery boy'—he taught me a lesson that's made a difference. All my life!

Now when I look at a young trainee or ambitious manager, this is the trait I look for above all else. How does he behave with his team? How well does he know the folks who work for him? How does he treat the ordinary people around him? Show me a guy who's terrific with people, who 'looks up' to his subordinates and I'll show you a star. Those unsung heroes we tend to take for granted, they will ensure he succeeds!

You could have had the finest education. You may be a master in your chosen field. You could be a senior manager. But if you really want to succeed, you need to learn to work with a team. You need to learn to respect people. That is perhaps the most critical skill for success. At work. And in life.

It's a lesson I learnt several years ago. And haven't forgotten it. And yes, the delivery boy's name, I later discovered, was Velu. I haven't forgotten that either.

In our lives, we tend to look up all the time at our superiors. We seldom find time for those 'lowly folks' who are looking up at us. To tell the true character of a person, just observe how he behaves with ordinary folks.

Leadership Lessons from Michelle Obama

Barack Obama's incredible journey to the White House has been well chronicled and is now part of popular lore. And if you tracked the Obama family's move into the White House, you might recall several interesting stories. Their train journey into Washington. The installation of a basketball post for the President to practise his slam dunk. The arrival of the Portuguese water dog, Bo. And more.

My favourite Obama story, however, is not about the President. It's about the first lady, Michelle Obama.

Time reported that soon after they moved into the White House, Michelle sent an email to her staff of advisors inviting them to a meeting in one of the many conference rooms in the White House. And as the team of policy advisors and communication experts walked in at the appointed hour, they were surprised by what they saw in the room.

Inside the meeting room was an army of people. Michelle had called in the entire household staff of the White House. Cooks and maids. Plumbers and electricians. Gardeners and janitors. Relatively insignificant people, seemingly unimportant folks but people nevertheless. People who kept the wheels running in the White House.

'This is my team that came with me from Chicago,' said Michelle, pointing to her team of advisors. 'And this is my team that works here already,' she went on, pointing to the household staff assembled in the room. And then for an hour or so, they mingled, with Michelle ensuring that everyone got a chance to meet everyone else.

Now you'll agree that inviting all the cooks and gardeners and the rest of the household staff was a nice gesture. But wait, there's more. Here's what Michelle said to her senior advisors: 'I want you to know that a year from now, you won't be judged based on whether they know your name. You'll be judged based on whether you know theirs.'

And that is a terrific lesson in people management. For Michelle's team. For all of us.

True leaders know the importance of focusing their lives and efforts on their team, rather than on themselves. When you have the power and the position, it is inevitable that you will be known by everyone on your team, wherever they may be. It's foolish to believe that your fame is your handiwork. It just comes with the job.

Learning to focus on others, showing that you value them, demonstrating genuine concern for people in the frontline—now *those* are the true hallmarks of great leaders. Do you know the name of the man who cleans your office? Do you know the name of the security guard who smiles and salutes you every morning? Do you?

Knowing the name is not the big deal. It's the ability, nay the habit, of turning the spotlight away from yourself and on to others, that matters. When the spotlight is on you, you can preen and walk about feeling good, but you will be blinded by the light, unable to see the faces around you. Turn the lights the other way and you will notice—very clearly—the smiles and the frowns, the joy and the despair on the faces around you. And the true test of leadership has got to be how well you know your team. Not how well your team knows you.

Dale Carnegie was right. In his immortal advice on winning friends and influencing people, here's what he said: 'You can make more friends in two months by becoming more interested in other people than you can in two years by trying to get people interested in you.'

Make a beginning. Get to know the cleaner in your office. The salesman in Siliguri. The maintenance engineer in the factory. And occasionally do the Michelle Obama thing: Get the staff into a room. Thank them. Get to know them better.

Don't focus on yourself. Take care of your team. And

they'll take care of you. Far better than you possibly can yourself!

True leaders know the importance of focusing on their team, rather than on themselves. A year from now, you won't be judged based on whether they know your name. You'll be judged based on whether you know theirs.

X

FINDING BALANCE

The PepsiCo Chief and the Call from Coke

He runs the New York Marathon every year. He graduated from the US Naval Academy and rose to the rank of captain in the US Marine Corps. Among his several roles, he served as a guard in the White House during the regimes of President Nixon and President Ford. He then moved into the corporate world, climbed rapidly and, in 2001, became the chairman and CEO of PepsiCo. In 2006, he decided to relinquish his post in favour of his deputy. A decision that yet again affirmed the truth in that old saying: 'It's best to quit when people ask why, not why not.' Whichever way you look at it, Steve Reinemund, this marathon runner and White House guard-turned-PepsiCo chief, had a remarkable career.

What do you think he would list as the high point of his career? Would it be the steps he took to diversify PepsiCo's portfolio to include good-for-health stuff, a shift that clearly took it ahead in the race against Coke? Or would it be the fact that under his leadership, revenues grew by $9 billion dollars, net income rose by 70 per cent, earnings per share were up 80 per cent and PepsiCo's market cap exceeded $100 billion dollars? Or could it be his diversity agenda? Steve worked passionately to create a diverse, all-inclusive team that reflected the mix of customers the company served. Or would it be just the fact that he knew when to quit and make way for his second-in-command, unlike several leaders who get so attached to their power that they refuse to let go and stay far beyond their best-before dates?

Any one of these would have been a source of great pride and joy for most leaders. But it's interesting to hear Steve recall one of those 'unforgettable moments' from a remarkably achievement-laden life. One moment that I think will top his charts. Here it is:

It was a day like any other. As Steve looked out of the window of his corner-room office on to the sprawling lawns of the PepsiCo campus, the silence was interrupted by the ringing of the phone on his desk. He picked it up. On the line was the CEO of the Coca-Cola Company.

He was calling Steve to thank him for an enormous favour. Steve, of course, had no idea what the favour was. It seems a packet containing some highly confidential Coca-Cola documents had been wrongly delivered to PepsiCo, instead of to Coke. And without it even being opened, the PepsiCo staff had immediately redirected it to Coke.

Well, Steve had no idea about this. After hanging up, he called his administration manager to find out more. And he was told yes indeed a packet meant for Coke had accidentally arrived at PepsiCo's office. And just two people knew about it: the woman handling the incoming mail, and her manager. In their wisdom, they decided that the right thing to do was to just send it to the correct addressee. In this case, the Coca-Cola Company. That's all. No long hours spent thinking what should be done. No asking for advice. No fuss.

Needless to say, Steve was proud of his team. Which is why I think this moment will remain special, even years later. Because this is not just about share gains or increases in market cap but about the building of an organization. Of an organization that won, by doing the right thing. At all times.

It's one thing to have a vision for the business, quite another to see it actually work. One thing to define values, another to see the organization live by them!

We all set values to live by but when it comes to the crunch, when push comes to shove—are we willing to live by them? The rivalry between Coke and Pepsi is legendary, and they have waged several hard battles around the world in their fight for a larger share of the consumer's throat and wallet. And yet, when some potentially explosive data about Coke landed inadvertently in Pepsi's lap—data that could have given them a competitive edge—the folks at Pepsi just did 'the right thing'.

Would you? Would your organization? Would that salesman or that despatch clerk or that pushy award-winning sales manager behave the same way as the woman at PepsiCo did that fateful day? Many of us swear by values such as honesty and integrity but when the rubber meets the road, do we stand up to scrutiny? When a mail meant for someone else lands in your inbox, can you resist the temptation to peek into it?

Or do you justify it by saying it's all right? After all you did not get it by fraudulent means. It doesn't really matter how it reached you. If it's not meant for you, well it's not meant for you. And it's interesting how we often redefine what's right—or wrong—based on our convenience.

Great leaders and great organizations are built on strong fundamentals. On a no-compromise adherence to a stated value system. Adherence by all—not just by some people. Adherence at all times—not just when it's convenient.

The real strength of character in the Pepsi story is reflected not just in the fact that the parcel reached its rightful owner, but in the fact that it was done without any fuss. There were no long meetings to decide the right course of action. The manager didn't check with her boss (and his boss and his boss's boss). Just two people in that large organization knew about it. And they just did what they thought—no, what they *knew*—was the right thing.

I think that's a great lesson to learn for individuals and for organizations. Values are not what are written on the office walls or on the first slide of the PowerPoint presentation to investors. Values are real-life responses of the people in the organization, to the challenges and temptations they face every day. Your personal values are not just what you espouse. It's how you behave and react in the face of temptation, under pressure, even when you know that no one else would know.

Often, our decision on what's the right thing to do is influenced by what we think is the probability of being caught out. 'What can we get away with?' seems to be the uppermost thought. Not 'What's the right thing?' If the folks at PepsiCo had opened that packet and dived into the secrets inside, no one would have known. Least of all Coke. The folks at Atlanta would have been left wondering about the mystery of the missing parcel. That's all.

What really matters is not what you do when the world is watching. It's what you do when no one is watching! Perhaps the packet contained secrets that could have helped Pepsi win a share point or pre-empt a competitive launch. Opening it may have created a market opportunity. Perhaps. But it would have destroyed an organization. Slowly, but surely.

What would you do if it were you, or your organization? What would you do if that envelope of secret opportunities mistakenly landed on your desk? Ah! That's easy. Of course, you wouldn't open it! That's what we all say.

The real question is this: What did you do the last time it happened? When your values were tested, when you had an opportunity to gain (albeit unfairly), when you knew you wouldn't get caught—yeah, what did you do?

Time to do some soul-searching. And time to ensure that we are all creating organizations where when the envelope meant for our competitor lands in the inbox, the despatch clerk knows what's the right thing to do. And not only does she know what's the right thing, she just goes ahead and does it!

Your personal values are not just what you espouse. It's how you behave and react in the face of temptation, under pressure, even when you know no one else would know.

Enough. Do You Have It?

If you are in the funds and investments business, you've probably heard of John Bogle. John is the founder and CEO of the Vanguard Mutual Fund Group, and also the creator of the world's first index fund. In his latest book, John tells an interesting story about Joseph Heller, author of the best-selling *Catch 22*.

A mutual friend took Heller to a party at a billionaire's home in New York. It was a fabulous evening and the generous host—a hedge fund manager—ensured that everyone was having a great time. The friend turned to Heller and said: 'Do you realize that our host probably makes more money in a day than you have made in a lifetime from your book?' Nodding his head slowly and sipping his wine, Joseph replied, 'Yes. But I have something he will never have.'

'What?' said the friend. And Joseph replied: 'Enough.'

I loved the story and as I read the book (appropriately

titled *Enough: True Measures of Money, Business, and Life*, my mind went back to Maslow and his famed hierarchy of needs. I thought of his pyramid and wondered if 'enough' figures anywhere in it. Self-actualization seems a fairly complex phrase for a simple enough word. Enough.

We all have our definitions of success, our secret list of desires. Wealth. Power. Fame. And more . . . Very few of us, if any, have 'enough' on that list.

What makes people happy? Money, love, health, respect? More of each of these? Or some magic combination of all of these? It's good to remember that true happiness comes not from getting (and wanting) more but from being satisfied with what you get. From knowing that enough is, well, enough. As a wise man put it, you don't have to be successful to be happy. Happiness can make you a success.

Wanting more puts us on a never-ending ride. Like a roller coaster whose operator has vanished—there's no one to switch it off! It starts off as a fun ride but not being able to get off means it's not fun any more. Look around and you will probably see several 'successful' people who have all it takes—except enough!

That money is not the secret to happiness has been well documented. You need enough of it, sure, but beyond a point it ceases to matter. So what really matters? What makes people happy? The magazine *American Psychologist* identified three factors, the three things you need to have in some measure to be truly happy. Call it the ACE trilogy if you will. The three needs are:

Autonomy: the freedom to do as you please

Connectivity: the ability to stay in touch with friends and dear ones

Execute competence: the opportunities to put to use your special talents and abilities

So the next time you contemplate a career move or worry about your bank balance, it may be a good idea to take stock of your ACE score. The problem is that in our quest for more and more, we tend to ignore what really matters. The freedom to do what your mind desires, the chance to spend time with the people you like, and the chance to do what you are really good at. If you have these, in some measure, you probably have enough.

Greed is at the heart of a lot of our problems. Perhaps it's time to say—enough. Time perhaps for each of us to define our own 'enoughs'. And discover true wealth and happiness.

We all have our definitions of success, our secret list of desires. Wealth. Power. Fame. And more . . . Very few of us, if any, have 'enough' on that list.

Pig. And Other Games People Play

Once when I was in Chennai, a friend told me about a game of dice he used to play in his childhood, and how the lessons he learnt from that game many, many years ago are still relevant. It's a game called Pig. I hadn't heard of it or played it ever. But as I heard about it, I found it quite fascinating!

The game goes like this: two players, two dice. The first player starts by throwing the dice; the face value that appears on the dice is the number of runs he scores. He throws the dice again, and again, and keeps adding to his score with every throw. If the same number appears on both dice, it's a bonus and the score doubles (so a 3 and 3 gets you 12 runs). And you go on throwing the dice, and accumulating runs. However, if you get a 1 and 1, then you are out. And your score gets reset to zero. And the next guy then takes his turn. At any stage, a player can choose to declare—and ask the other player to start throwing. At the end of five innings, the guy with the higher total score wins.

Sounds simple. And fun. Right?

Now here's the tricky bit. As my friend recalls, it would be great fun throwing the dice and scoring runs and watching your score climb. And then if you got a 5 and 5 or a 6 and 6, there would be jubilation. And as their score went past the 100-run mark, it wasn't unusual for him—or his brother—to start admiring his own skill, his inner genius, which was resulting in those tall scores. The thought that the next throw could be a 1 and 1—which would mean that they'd be back to zero—would never cross their mind.

And then inevitably, 1 and 1 would appear. Reducing their score to nought. Leading to anguish on one face, delight on the other. The poor soul whose score was reduced to zero would rue his fate, and passionately have you believe that he was just about to declare. He had decided, he'd say, that it would be his last throw. All to no avail. And then the other person would start his innings. Needless to say, he would hardly have learnt a lesson from his rival! 'It didn't quite occur to us,' recalls my friend, 'that it might be a good idea to set a target in our mind, predetermine the number of throws, and then declare.'

And while I had said to him that I had never played Pig,

I quickly realized that it looked like a game I had indeed played, several times. In a casino. In the stock market. In life. When the going is good, we let greed get the better of us. The stock market index climbs, and climbs higher, and we cheer and admire our stock-picking abilities. We don't always declare—or exit—because the thought that a '1 and 1' could be just around the corner doesn't quite occur to us. We push that uncomfortable thought out of our minds.

Which is probably why if you listen to someone who's just been to a casino, he will delight in telling you how at one stage he had won over a thousand bucks. Yeah, *at one stage*. Only to lose it all.

In life, you need a plan, which not only includes how much you want to make but also when you want to exit. If you are not careful, if you allow greed to rule you, a '1 and 1' will appear and bring your score back to zero.

And the problem in the game of dice—as in the game of life—is that most times we aren't just looking at our scores, but trying to be one up on the other guy. That's what feeds the greed and keeps us running. Our targets are not about how much we need but how we should have more than the other guy. And that is a recipe for disaster. In Pig. In life.

Cricketers face the Pig effect too. It's the all-too-familiar story of a great cricketer, who garners fans and glory and then, despite declining ability, holds on for one more game, one more endorsement contract, one more record . . . only to lose it all, as he gets pushed into oblivion. Vijay Merchant, the legendary Indian cricketer, had advice for cricketers that holds good for all of us: 'Quit when people will ask "Why?" and not "Why not?"'

Good to take some lessons away from the game called Pig, into the larger game of life. Set targets for yourself. Know when to call it quits. Worry about your own score, not about the other guy's. When the tide is in your favour, resist the temptation to boast about your surfing skills. And learn to keep greed out.

We all tend to be greedy pigs, I thought to myself! And suddenly figured how the game got its name.

Have a plan, which includes not only how much you need to make but also when you need to call it quits.

Smelling the Coffee

There's a quarterly event I secretly look forward to with great eagerness—the reunion lunch of my batchmates, the gang of IIMA 86! It wasn't always like this but as the years have rolled by, the sense of nostalgia and belonging has grown quite dramatically.

It's a relaxed lunch where a group of us—usually twenty-five or so—get together to catch up, laugh, exchange notes and reminisce about the good old days. The presence of spouses ensures that the discussion doesn't get too heavy on stock markets and boardroom battles; there's usually as much chatter on the latest Bollywood release, the kids' homework and the new restaurant in town.

Our hairlines have receded, our waistlines are bulging and two decades in the corporate world have seen all of us go down different paths. But, as every quarterly rendezvous seems to confirm, the reunion lunch has the uncanny ability to somehow shrink the distances we have travelled, and transport us back to the time when we were all thrown together in the red-brick-walled confines of one of the best places to be in the world, the campus of the Indian Institute of Management in Ahmedabad. At the reunion, nobody is a CEO or a billionaire. We are just the same young fellas of the class of '86. All excited, eager-eyed, in hawai chappals, unshaven, even unbathed!

The life stories are interesting. One of our batchmates is a top cop in the city. A man doing a fabulous job, sans reward, of maintaining law and order and ensuring that we all sleep well. There's another guy who gave up a lucrative job with a consulting major to do something on his own—so he could spend more time with wife and family. (Know what prompted it? His daughter complained to her teacher that her Papa was not spending enough time with her and that he was on his BlackBerry all the time at home.)

I've noticed that at these lunches, while the conversations are wide-ranging, there's very little interest in discussing individual progress reports. That's a complete no-no. Thank God for that!

I wonder if we were lucky to have graduated before the great investment banking boom of the 1990s. We chose jobs that excited us, not the ones that paid the most or offered postings in exotic foreign locations. We chased our dreams. And while we all find our eyes popping in disbelief every time we hear about the astronomical starting salaries at that well-known institute of management in western India, we are probably a happier, more contented lot. It's so much nicer to be able to remember the two years at IIMA for the time spent there, rather than for a starting salary.

Reminds me of a little story. You've probably heard it but there's a message in it for all of us. Perhaps even more so for that young fast-track i-banker jetting across time zones, buying his next swanky apartment, upgrading to a new BMW and delighting in telling his friends about how he and his wife briefly caught up with each other at Frankfurt airport last week.

The story goes that a group of alumni, highly established in their careers, got together to visit their old university professor. Conversation soon turned into complaints about stress at work and life. Offering his guests coffee, the professor went to the kitchen and returned with a large pot of coffee and an assortment of cups: porcelain, plastic, glass, some plain-looking and some quite exquisite. He then asked them to help themselves to hot coffee. When all the students had a cup of coffee in hand, the professor said: 'If you notice, all the nice-looking, expensive cups are taken, leaving behind the plain and cheap ones. While it is but normal for you to want only the best for yourselves, that is the source of your problems and your stress. What all of you really wanted was coffee, not the cup, but you consciously went for the better cups and are eyeing each other's cups.'

'Now, if Life is coffee, then the jobs, money and position in society are the cups. They are just tools to hold and contain Life, they don't change the quality of Life. At times, by concentrating only on the cup, we fail to enjoy the coffee in it.'

Think about it. And don't forget to smell the coffee!

What we really need is the coffee. But what we keep searching for are better-looking cups.

What's Better than Winning a Gold Medal? Losing It!

Have you heard of Lawrence Lemieux?

Probably not. He's one of those Olympic heroes who never won a medal. And yet, his name is indelibly etched on the list of all-time greats. On the list of men and women who, in their own ways, epitomize the Olympic spirit.

Lemieux, a Canadian sailor, grew up dreaming of Olympic glory. Years of struggle, sacrifice and sailing were finally rewarded when he was selected to represent his country in the Finn class sailing event at the Seoul Olympics, 1988.

The big day arrived on 24 September 1988. The sailing events were being held in Pusan, about 450 km away from Seoul. The competitors set sail in fine weather but conditions got worse as the race progressed, and wind speeds climbed from under 15 knots to nearly 35 knots. The waters got choppy, the boats wobbled, the crew was under threat . . . and a race was on.

Halfway through the race, Lemieux was in second place, doing rather well despite the adverse weather conditions. As he gazed into the distance, his mind probably saw visions of an Olympic medal. The realization of a lifelong dream seemed near, very near. Stay focused, push yourself that extra bit, go for it, this is the moment you've worked so hard for . . . Lemieux was egging himself on.

But then, looking into the distance, he saw something else too. Across the choppy waters, two men were struggling for dear life, clinging on to a capsized boat. They were Joseph Chan and Siew Shaw Her, two sailors from the Singapore team who were competing in another sailing event, the 470 class. Their boat had gone out of control, they were injured and their lives were in danger.

In an instant, Lemieux decided what he had to do, what appeared to him to be the right thing.

Quickly changing course, he headed towards the two sailors in distress. With considerable difficulty, he managed to rescue Joseph first and bring him on to his own boat, which itself seemed close to capsizing. He then rescued an injured and bleeding Siew, dragging him against the force of strong currents. With the two men on his boat, relatively safe, he waited for the rescue patrol, which soon came and took the two injured men away for medical attention.

Lemieux wasn't finished though. Not yet. He decided

to get back to his race. But he had lost too much time in saving two lives. From his earlier second position, he had now slipped to number twenty-two in a field of thirty-two competitors. Lemieux's dream of an Olympic medal was over, but at the medal ceremony, Juan Samaranch, president of the International Olympic Committee, presented Lemieux the Pierre de Coubertin medal or the True Medal of Sportsmanship and said, 'By your sportsmanship, self-sacrifice and courage, you embody all that is right with the Olympic ideal.'

In our lives, we often find ourselves in situations like the one that Lawrence Lemieux faced. Our sailboats are different, the winds vary, the cries for help sound different but the challenge is the same—a conflict of personal goals versus the larger good. Can we tell what's really important? Will we willingly sacrifice personal glory for larger goals? Can we tell what really matters from what seems to matter?

It is often said that the road to the top in the corporate world is littered with corpses. Friends, colleagues and associates are quite nonchalantly sacrificed at the altar of personal glory. What is it worth? What would you rather be remembered for—getting a promotion ahead of a colleague, amassing a fatter bank balance, winning the top job? Or for making a difference to someone else's life?

Gaining market share or clinching a major deal may get you into the corner office faster but when, in your twilight years, you sit on your rocking chair and think back . . . What would you like to be remembered for? What do you *think* you will be remembered for?

Lemieux, now long retired, is a successful and much-sought-after coach. People from all walks of life want to hear his story. To remind themselves of a basic lesson in life, to be reminded what being a winner is all about. 'Good thing I didn't win a medal,' he says. 'If I had, I would've been all but forgotten by now!'

Many, many people have won Olympic medals—an outstanding achievement undoubtedly. But few, very few, have achieved what Lemieux has.

Perhaps we need to redefine true success for ourselves. What is our gold medal? How do we react when we see our own sailors-in-distress? The question is not what you would do if you were in Lemieux's place—the question is what have you done when you have so often been in that place?

Medals don't matter. Mettle does!

Will you sacrifice personal glory for larger, selfless goals? Can you tell what really matters from what seems to matter? What would you rather be remembered for? Getting a promotion ahead of a colleague? Or making a difference to someone else's life?

Work–life Balance and the Waugh Brothers

It was the stuff parental dreams are made of. To have your child play for the country would be a dream come true for most. And to have two of your sons—twins at that—play for your country? Well, that would be really special!

And so it was with Mrs and Mr Waugh in Australia. As their twin sons—Steve and Mark—plundered runs and made waves in Australian first-class cricket, the great parental dream began building up. They longed for the day when both their sons would play for Australia.

Steve made his debut first. There was joy in the Waugh home, and the desire to see Mark join him only grew stronger. The parents looked forward to the day when Mark too would get picked. And then it happened. Coming home after nets one day, Steve announced to his parents that Mark had been picked for the upcoming Ashes Test. The Waughs were delighted. 'Let's party tonight,' said the mother. After all, this was a special event, worthy of celebration! How many mothers have seen both sons play together in the national team?

The Waugh backyard was the venue for the bash. Pride and bonhomie combined with food and wine to create the perfect evening. As the proud mother refilled glasses of wine, she casually asked Steve: 'So who did the selectors drop to make way for Mark?'

With the calm that was to become legendary in later years, Steve replied: 'Me!'

Phew! Life's like that. Good news often comes mixed with the bad. You win some. You lose some. You get a gift-wrapped goodie. For a price.

I recall the words of K.V. Kamath, then the head honcho of ICICI Bank, as he addressed a gathering of industry leaders in Mumbai. In a panel discussion along with two professors from Harvard Business School, Mr Kamath poo-poohed the idea of work–life balance. He said it was a nice ideal, but not something he'd recommend to a young high-performance manager.

You need to focus on work, he said. Slog, make an impact, sweat it out, work harder to meet business goals . . . and life will take care of itself. And then, hopefully you will find the magical work–life balance. But trying to find that balance very early in your life could mean that you miss out on both fronts. Loser at work, not much joy in life either.

Something we would all do well to remember. To get something, you've got to give up something. That's how it will be in the beginning. After a while, if you are lucky, you will find the balance you are looking for.

Want to lose weight? You can, but you will need to say NO to your favourite sweets. Once you sacrifice the sweets and get your weight under control, you can indulge your sweet tooth. Weight loss and *gajar ka halwa* can co-exist!

Want to climb the corporate ladder? Slog. Work long hours. Forget weekends. As success sets in, you can start to discover fancy holiday spots. And the golf course. And your daughter's dance debut. And weekends too. But insisting on having both, right at the beginning, would almost certainly mean getting neither.

As the Waugh brothers have shown, Mr Kamath is probably right. After that famous debut game where Steve made way for Mark, the brothers went on to play for several years for Australia. Winning games, laurels and a couple of World Cups too.

The Waugh dream did come true. But imagine if the parents had insisted on both brothers making their debut at the same time, in the same game, it may have never happened. Without realizing, we often do that. We want that promotion AND we want to leave the office at 5.30 p.m. We want to lose weight AND we want that second helping of dessert. It just doesn't work that way. Not in cricket. Not in life.

Whatever your goals, go forth and work to make them come true. And remember Mr Kamath's words. You must be ready to pay the price!

Win some. Lose some. To get something, you've got to give up something.

XI

TAKE ACTION

Begin. And End. Nothing Else Matters

Sometimes a simple little snippet can point to larger life lessons. Sample this:

'Aoccrdnig to a rseearch at Cmabrigde Uinervtisy, it deosnt mttaer in waht oredr the ltteers in a wrod are. The olny iprmoatnt tihng is taht the frist and lsat ltteer be in the rghit pcale. The rset can be a taotl mses and you can sitll raed it wouthit a porbelm. Tihs is bcuseae the huamn mnid deos not raed ervey ltteer by istlef, but the wrod as a wlohe.'

The road to success in life too is quite similar. Getting started is key. And learning to finish tasks is priceless. The rest is, well, commentary.

I like the old saying that you don't have to be great to get started but you have to get started to be great. You can have the most fabulous ideas, some great plans, and the intent may never be in doubt. But all that is worth nothing if you don't get started. We often hesitate to get started, waiting for everything to be in place. But remember that everything seldom falls into place!

Unfinished tasks are the biggest contributors to stress in the workplace. Learn to finish tasks. Get them out of the way. If something is worth doing, it's worth doing badly at first. Successful people make it a habit to finish what they have started.

So if you have a big idea or a secret dream, take that first step. Today! Want to become a best-selling author? Write the first chapter. Today! And take a look at your unfinished tasks, your to-do list. Resolve to complete at least one of those tasks. Today!

Do that and see the difference. Life will begin to make a lot more sense.

Two keys to success—get started, and learn to finish. The rest is, well, commentary.

Of Wake-up Calls and Snooze Buttons . . .

The loudest noise today is the ringing of the wake-up call. When you hear of a young friend who's had a heart attack, you know it's a wake-up call for you to start that jog, to get on to the treadmill and to get back into fitness mode.

When you hear of the crash of the biggies on Wall Street, you know it's a wake-up call for Indian banking majors who've been busy spamming mobile phones with 'please may I offer you a no-questions-asked loan' calls.

When you hear of smells-like-Enron controversies, you know it's a wake-up call for company boards and CEOs to take corporate governance seriously.

When you read about how the distance between an argument and the divorce court is getting shorter in metros, you know it's a wake-up call to pay more attention to your relationships, to work on making your marriage work.

And when you hear about the New York i-banker (he of that fancy fat bonus last year) suddenly going into depression following a pink slip, you know it's a wake-up call to get your priorities right and find balance in your life's goals.

But hey, wait a minute! What do we do when we hear these wake-up calls? Our typical response to all these signals is something like this: We talk about it animatedly with our friends. (Oh yes, these make for excellent bar conversation!) We then resolve we must do something about it immediately. Soon. Tomorrow. And, of course, tomorrow never comes.

Yet, despite the constant blaring of all these wake-up calls, why is it that most of us don't really do anything about them? Two reasons, I suspect.

First, a false sense of invincibility, the 'it-can't-happen-to-me' syndrome. We always think it only happens to others. The heart attack. The bankruptcy. The pink slip. The broken marriage. We don't realize that 'they' too are people like us. Or were, at least.

Second, what I like to call the 'hit-the-snooze-button' syndrome. The temptation to put off action until a bit later. And then a little later.

The exercise regimen you promised yourself doesn't quite get started. The day you hear about your friend's heart attack, you say you will start the next day. That doesn't happen. You then promise yourself you'll do it after the Diwali binges. Then, after you come back from that business trip. Then from the first of January, promise! It never, never happens. Until it's too late!

CEOs and company boards are like that too. Must set it right next quarter, they say. Not this one, the next. One good quarter, and we'll take care of it. Next financial year . . . And then, a Satyam happens. The truth is, we've all got used to the wonderful snooze button on our alarm calls. To get up at 6.30 a.m., we set the alarm for 6 a.m. We wake up, stretch hand, reach alarm, hit snooze . . . 6.10 a.m. We wake up, hit snooze . . . 6.20 a.m. Ditto 6.30 a.m. Finally wake up. Research shows that those thirty minutes are a complete waste. You don't really sleep in those three ten-minute intervals. And you don't put that time to productive use either. All that the snooze button does is to give us a feeling that it can wait. And we start thinking that everything can wait. Our minds develop their own versions of the snooze button.

So what happens is that every time we hear a wake-up call, we reach out for the snooze button, which isn't really there. But it's taken permanent residence in our minds.

Do yourself a favour. Cut off the snooze button. From your cellphone, your alarm clock, your mind, your life. Get up when the alarm rings. Don't hit snooze. When you hear a wake-up call, wake up. Make it a habit.

You'll find many benefits of this one change in your

behaviour. You will sleep well. You will create more time for yourself every morning. And most importantly, when those critical wake-up calls come along in your life, you'll take action.

You'll wake up. Before it's too late.

Forget the snooze button. When you hear a wake-up call, wake up!

The Second-best Time to Do Anything

Do you often look back and wish you had done things differently? Do you, for instance, wish you had cultivated the reading habit as a child so you'd be a better-read person today? Wish you had played a sport and stayed with it beyond college so you'd be a fitter person today? Wish you had gone easy on sweets so you wouldn't be an obese diabetic today? Wish you had told your parents and spouse and kids how very much you loved them?

Or are you the kind of person who constantly sees change in the future tense? 'I will give up sweets—after Diwali'. Or 'I will spend more time with the family—once we wrap up the annual business plans.' Or 'I will quit and do what I have always wanted to—after I have that magic number in my bank account.'

You will do well to remember the wisdom contained in an old Chinese proverb: 'The best time to plant a tree was twenty years ago. The second-best time is now!' It's up to us to make the most of now!

Business gurus and spiritual leaders have all talked about the power of now. The power of living in the present versus the futility of living in a past that's gone or dreaming of an imaginary future.

Often, our excuse for not acting is either that the best time has passed or is still to come. And our quest for the 'right time' helps mask our lethargy, and fuels our tendency to procrastinate. Success comes to those who live in the present, who seize the moment. What's gone is gone, no point living in regret. And the future? Well, as the saying goes, tomorrow never comes. So whatever it is that you wish to do, do it today. Do it now. Make use of the second-best time. Remember, it's never too late to become what you might have been.

Want to learn a new skill? Start lessons today. Want to lose weight? Start exercises today. Want to have better relationships? Reach out and hug your loved ones today. Whatever it is you want, make a beginning. Today.

Today is the tomorrow you thought of yesterday. This might sound somewhat philosophical but it's for real! When you start living in the present, that's when you unleash the power that's within you. And sure enough, twenty years from today, you'll be glad you planted that tree!

Here then is a question for you. If you knew today that

you had only six months to live, what would you do? Come on, think. What would you do in the last six months of your life?

Spend more time with the family? Watch Manchester United take on Chelsea with your son? Listen to your daughter talk about the latest episode of *How I Met Your Mother*? Take a leisurely walk with your wife, hands firmly clasped, wind blowing her hair across her face, just like on your first date? Set off on a holiday with the family perhaps? To the hills or beaches, wildlife sanctuaries or great monuments. So much to see, so much to do. And so little time.

And you would perhaps spend a day with your mother? Reliving memories of the days gone by. Your first day at school. How she made your favourite *bhindi sabzi*—and made you believe that bhindi sharpens your mathematical skills! And how worried she was when you came home with a swollen nose when a cricket ball smacked you in the face. You slept that night; she didn't.

Six months to go. What would you do differently?

Would you get up early every morning and read those ten books you've always wanted to but never quite found the time for? Or would you finally get down to writing the book that's been brewing inside you, waiting to be written?

Perhaps you'd want to catch up with friends. School-mates you grew up with—but grew away from. Old neighbours, who huddled up with you to watch *Chhayageet* on Wednesday nights and cheered with you as you watched Sunil Gavaskar—in black and white—hammer Arthur Barrett in a memorable 86-run knock at Wankhede Stadium.

And you'd perhaps want to write letters and send e-mails. To thank people for what they've meant to you. Or say sorry to people you may have hurt, unintentionally. Amazing how an apology can lift a huge burden off your chest. You always knew it, but never got around to it.

What else would you do if you knew you had only six months to go?

Perhaps audition with a TV channel to anchor a show? After all, you've spent several evenings convinced that you could do a better job than the lady on air. And you'd gladly swap your cushy corporate job for a day as a commentator in India's T20 game.

And you'd perhaps want to spend an entire day with your children, quickly sharing with them the lessons you've learnt in your life. All about what they don't teach you at Harvard or IIMA.

And you'd want to spend a day with your wife, watching the mushy English film she's been wanting to watch (and you've been avoiding for some twenty years); eating the pasta she's been longing for (and you've been avoiding for twenty years) and finally reassuring her with those three magical words she's been wanting to hear just one more time (but you haven't bothered to say them for twenty years).

With six months to go, what would you do? Remember, no man on his deathbed ever said 'I wish I'd spent more time in the office.'

Whatever your answers, here's the real lesson. Whatever it is that you want to do in the last six months of your life, do it now. Today. Because truth is, you never get to know when you have only six months to go. So live every day, as if it were the start of your 'last six months'.

Take that holiday. Watch that game with your son. Listen to your daughter's stories. Take that walk with your wife. Spend that day with your mom. Read. Travel. Play. Enjoy. Live!

Whatever you fancy, do it now. Don't wait for those last six months, because you will never know when the countdown begins. Live every day to the fullest. So what would you do if you had only six months to live? Whatever your answer, just remember one thing. Your time starts now.

If you knew today that you had only six months to live, what would you do? Whatever it is, do it now. Today. Because truth is, you never get to know when you have only six months to go.

Acknowledgements

I feel blessed to have had a wonderful family from whom I learnt my first lessons and habits in life. I was fortunate to have had some truly caring teachers who encouraged me to dream, and taught me a whole lot more than History or Chemistry. And I have been privileged to have had some terrific friends, and outstanding colleagues. And watching them all, working with them, and sharing moments of joy and despair with them—have taught me valuable lessons and helped shape the person I am. If you are friend, family, colleague or teacher—you may not find your name mentioned, but you would recognize that this book would not have been possible without you. You made a difference to my life. Thank you for that!

This book is really a collection of stories that I have picked up over the years, working alongside some truly remarkable people. And while I learnt something in every organization, every team, there was something magical about going to work wearing a Pepsi shirt. The passion, the fierce will to win and the fabulous team spirit have been strong influences. Old jungle saying: You can take a man out of Pepsi. You can't take Pepsi out of the man.

I'd like to thank Suman Sinha—mentor, friend, philosopher, critic and guide. I've had the pleasure of knowing Suman for over two decades now—and his passion, his focus on building teams and growing managers, and his zealous advocacy of values—have all been hugely inspiring. Forget B-schools. Proud to call myself an alumnus of the Suman School of Management.

From the time a colleague lent me a set of Brian Tracy audiotapes, I have benefited hugely from listening to a wide range of inspirational gurus including Jim Rohn, Zig Ziglar, Tony Robbins and of course, Brian himself. I would like to thank them for strengthening my fundamental belief in the goodness—nay greatness—of all human beings.

R. Gopalakrishnan has been an inspiration and a role model, in all his roles: as an outstanding professional, fantastic leader, best-selling author, great teacher and a fabulous human being. Thanks RG for consenting to write the foreword to this book. It means more to me than you'll ever know!

It was Mahesh Peri who read my blog and felt the messages there could be of interest to a larger audience. And thus was born my monthly column in Careers 360.

I'd like to thank Mahesh and the team at Careers 360 for providing me a platform to share my stories. Their support—and the readers' response to my column—have been hugely motivating.

Thanks also to Heather Adams, Debasri RC and the team at Penguin, for their ideas and support—and for making it happen.

And finally, a big thank you to the three people in my life who mean the world to me, and make my world a better place. My wife and children have been my biggest critics and my biggest fans—and my own little test lab for my stories and theories. Savvy, Abs and Tuts: this one's for you. And sorry if I wasn't listening when you were saying something to me yesterday. As you can see, I was probably thinking about a new story.

Promise, I'll try harder. Starting today!